THE MAD® BATHROOM COMPANION

TURD IN A SERIES

Also available from MAD Books

The MAD Monster Book of Horrifying Clichés

MAD About the Mob

MAD About Super Heroes

MAD Neumanisms

The MAD Bathroom Companion Number Two

The MAD Gross Book

The MAD Bathroom Companion

MAD About TV

MAD About the Movies—Special Warner Bros. Edition

THE MAD® BATHROOM COMPANION

TURD IN A SERIES

By "The Usual Gang of Idiots"

Edited by Nick Meglin & John Ficarra

Introduction by Gilbert Gottfried

Published by MAD Books. An imprint of E.C. Publications, Inc., 1700 Broadway, New York, NY 10019. A division of Warner Bros.—An AOL Time Warner Company.

ISBN 1-4012-0055-9

Printed in Canada

First edition
10 9 8 7 6 5 4 3 2 1

Visit *MAD* online at www.madmag.com

CONTENTS

"Time Flies...Time Drags...(and Vice Versa)," by Stan Hart, illustrated by Paul Coker, Jr. (*MAD* #247)
"You Know You're in a Second Marriage When...," written and illustrated by Lloyd Gola (*MAD* #244)
"Interpreting the News," by Gary Alexander (*MAD* #163)
"Making Baseball Card Collections Complete," by Desmond Devlin, illustrated by John Pound (*MAD* #296)
"A *MAD* Look at Palm Reading," written and illustrated by Sergio Aragonés (*MAD* #145)
"Things You Can Do For Your Dog On His Birthday," written and illustrated by Paul Peter Porges (*MAD* #255)
"A *MAD* Look at Tarzan," by Don Edwing, illustrated by Jack Davis (*MAD* #161)
"TV Emmy Awards We'd Like to See," by Mike Snider, illustrated by Michael Montgomery (*MAD* #266)
"Snappy Answers to Stupid Bumper Stickers," by Larry Siegel, illustrated by Bob Clarke (*MAD* #252)
"The *MAD* Practical Driving Test," by Tom Koch, illustrated by Paul Coker, Jr. (*MAD* #256)
"While Clamming in New Jersey," written and illustrated by Don Martin (*MAD* #130)
"Fortune Cookies That Are Relevant," by Dick DeBartolo and Don Epstein (*MAD* #162)
"The Lighter Side of...," written and illustrated by Dave Berg (*MAD* #238)
"One Day on a Hike," written and illustrated by Don Martin (*MAD* #131)
"The Name Game of the Rich and Famous," by J. Prete, illustrated by Mort Drucker (*MAD* #286)
"A *MAD* Look at Some Widely Held Misconceptions," by Mike Snider, illustrated by Harvey Kurtzman (*MAD* #273)
"Spy vs. Spy," by Duck Edwing, illustrated by Bob Clarke (*MAD* #272)
"Odes to Appliances, Gadgets and Other Modern Conveniences," idea by Marilyn Atkins, written by Frank Jacobs, illustrated by George Woodbridge (*MAD* #269)
"Don Edwing Looks at Funerals," written and illustrated by Don Edwing (*MAD* #253)
"When 'Doublespeak' Takes Over Completely," by Frank Jacobs, illustrated by Sergio Aragonés (*MAD* #295)
"Patterns of Speech," idea by Max Brandel, illustrated by Bob Clarke (*MAD* #158)
"Specialized Nautilus Machines For Practical Everyday Activities," by Larry Siegel, illustrated by Al Jaffee (*MAD* #287)
"One Day in a Garage," written and illustrated by Don Martin (*MAD* #136)
"What It Will Be Like When Every Device 'Talks,'" by Dick DeBartolo, illustrated by Paul Coker, Jr. (*MAD* #251)
"*MAD*'s Alibis For All Occasions," by Tom Koch, illustrated by Jack Davis (*MAD* #272)
"More Ads We Never Got to See," by Dick DeBartolo, illustrated by Harry North (*MAD* #248)
"One Night in the Acme Ritz Central Arms Waldorf Plaza Statler Hilton Grand Hotel," written and illustrated by Don Martin (*MAD* #142)
"If Computers Are So Brilliant..." by Tom Koch, illustrated by George Woodbridge (*MAD* #258)
"A *MAD* Look at Amusement Parks," written and illustrated by Sergio Aragonés (*MAD* #146)
"Pastimes for Nerds," written and illustrated by Paul Peter Porges (*MAD* #256)
"Spy vs. Spy," by Duck Edwing, illustrated by Bob Clarke (*MAD* #274)
"The *MAD* People Watcher's Guide to an Airport," by Mike Snider, illustrated by Tom Bunk (*MAD* #299)
"Truth in Road Signs," by Dick DeBartolo, illustrated by Bob Clarke (*MAD* #260)
"The Lighter Side of...," written and illustrated by Dave Berg (*MAD* #253)
"*MAD*'s Aptitude Test Number One: Will You Make a Good Doctor?" by Frank Jacobs, illustrated by George Woodbridge (*MAD* #243)
"All You Need to Know You Learned in Nursery School," by Tom Koch, illustrated by Paul Coker, Jr. (*MAD* #296)
"If Famous Movies Were Made Into Comic Strips," written and illustrated by Russ Cooper (*MAD* #295)
"A *MAD* Guide to Social Behavior," by Chris Hart, illustrated by Bob Jones (*MAD* #289)
"One Day During a Cavalry Attack," written and illustrated by Don Martin (*MAD* #154)
"Laundromat Bingo," by Rurik Tyler, illustrated by Bob Clarke (*MAD* #260)
"*MAD* Mini-Movies Featuring the Fickle Finger of Fate," written and illustrated by Al Jaffee (*MAD* #269)

"The Startling Similarities Between Ancient Mythology & Modern Rock," by Desmond Devlin, illustrated by Rick Tulka (*MAD* #306)
"One Tuesday Morning," written and illustrated by Don Martin (*MAD* #155)
"What's in a Name? Part Two: Institutions," conceived by Max Brandel (*MAD* #164)
"Amazing Facts (and Surprising Discoveries) From the Human Genome DNA Project," by Mike Snider, illustrated by Paul Coker, Jr. (*MAD* #413)
"The *MAD* D.J. Primer," by Lou Silverstone, illustrated by Jack Davis (*MAD* #273)
"A *MAD* Look at Hunting," written and illustrated by Sergio Aragonés (*MAD* #155)
"Celebrity Sound Effects," written and illustrated by John Caldwell (*MAD* #302)
"Warning Labels of the Future Designed to Head Off Potential Lawsuits," by Dick DeBartolo, illustrated by Bob Clarke (*MAD* #301)
"Duck Edwing Hangs Out at the Mall," written and illustrated by Duck Edwing (*MAD* #309)
"Your *MAD* Horoscope," by John Ficarra (*MAD* #229)
"*MAD*'s Practical Joke Catalogue For Doctors," by Beppe Sabatini, illustrated by Al Jaffee (*MAD* #248)
"Old MacDonald," idea by Dan Lozer, written by Frank Jacobs, illustrated by Gerry Gersten (*MAD* #294)
"One Day on the Highway," written and illustrated by Don Martin (*MAD* #157)
"10 Little Candidates," by Frank Jacobs, illustrated by Paul Coker, Jr. (*MAD* #313)
"The Lighter Side of...," written and illustrated by Dave Berg (*MAD* #256)
"*MAD*'s Updated Book Titles," by William Garvin, illustrated by Bob Clarke (*MAD* #294)
"World Communism Close-Out Sale," by Mike Snider, illustrated by John Pound (*MAD* #299)
"How to End a Date Painlessly," written and illustrated by Paul Peter Porges (*MAD* #259)
"*MAD*'s Instant Movie Reviews," by Russ Cooper, illustrated by Gerry Gersten (*MAD* #305)
"Late One Night in a Waterfront Tavern," written and illustrated by Don Martin (*MAD* #158)
"When Roadside Signs Overlap," by Henry Clark, illustrated by George Woodbridge (*MAD* #308)
"Spy vs. Spy," by Duck Edwing, illustrated by Bob Clarke (*MAD* #273)
"Eavesdropper Shockers," by Mike Snider, illustrated by Bob Jones (*MAD* #294)
"The *MAD* Stages of...," written and illustrated by Rick Tulka (*MAD* #309)
"Guys You're Likely to Meet Before Mr. 'Right,'" by Mike Snider, illustrated by Alyse Newman (*MAD* #286)
"Rules for Games the Way They're Really Played," by Michael Goodwin, illustrated by Jack Davis (*MAD* #312)
"One Night in a Police Station," written and illustrated by Don Martin (*MAD* #165)
"A *MAD* Look at Fast Food," written and illustrated by Sergio Aragonés (*MAD* #272)
"New Uses For Old Batteries," written and illustrated by Al Jaffee (*MAD* #260)
"The Lighter Side of...," written and illustrated by Dave Berg (*MAD* #258)
"*MAD*'s Aptitude Test Number Four: Will You Make a Good Politician?" by Frank Jacobs, illustrated by George Woodbridge (*MAD* #246)
"Horrifying Political Clichés," by Frank Jacobs, illustrated by Paul Coker, Jr. (*MAD* #311)
"The *MAD* Travel Agency's Specialized Tours For You and Your Neurosis," by Stan Hart, illustrated by Harry North, Esq. (*MAD* #193)
"One Night in a Living Room," written and illustrated by Don Martin (*MAD* #159)
"More Obituaries for Merchandising Characters," by Frank Jacobs, illustrated by Bob Clarke (*MAD* #311)
"Stupid Pet Owner Tricks," written and illustrated by Paul Peter Porges (*MAD* #287)
"A *MAD* Peek Behind the Scenes on the Set of a Slasher Movie," by Dick DeBartolo, illustrated by Greg Theakston (*MAD* #293)
"Spy vs. Spy," by Duck Edwing, illustrated by Bob Clarke (*MAD* #277)
"*MAD* Magazine Reader's Competition," by Joe Raiola and Charlie Kadau (*MAD* #301)
"'Hey—Look Behind You!,'" by Mark D'Amico, illustrated by Al Jaffee (*MAD* #298)
"A *MAD* Look at Weddings," written and illustrated by Sergio Aragonés (*MAD* #160)
"Cause or Coincidence??," by Dan Birtcher, illustrated by George Woodbridge (*MAD* #306)
"How to Spice Up Your Video Will," by Jeff Kruse, illustrated by Tom Bunk (*MAD* #421)
"One Day With a Wishbone," written and illustrated by Don Martin (*MAD* #160)
"Drawn Out Dramas," illustrated throughout by Sergio Aragonés

Introduction

GEE, *The MAD Bathroom Companion*. Thinking about it leaves me totally flushed (sorry, I couldn't resist). This is a perfect idea because every time I go to the bathroom, I usually take an issue of *MAD* with me. I find the pages come in handy when I run out of toilet paper. Sometimes I'll use two pages at once, for that extra double-quilt comfort. Although, one time, the ink rubbed off, and I walked around all day with a picture of Alfred E. Neuman on my ass.

But enough about my regularity. I want to tell you about when I was a kid. Like many *MAD* readers, I guess my fascination with the magazine started when my mother bought me an issue (now you know why I still read at a first-grade level).

Reading *MAD*, I had many favorites. I was a big fan of Don Martin's work. His cartoons always had strange, made-up noises written in them, like "POIT!" and "FARRAPPGHT!" Then, of course, he would end them with a character being flattened by a piano, a boulder, etc. *MAD* published a few Don Martin books that I had to have, and I soon realized that 75% of the books were POIT! and FARRAPPGHT!

There was "The Lighter Side of..." cartoons by Dave Berg. I always liked Dave Berg's work, not because he was funny or hip. But because he was like that *un*hip uncle who would put a mop on his head and say, "Hey, look at me. Look at your Uncle Mel! I'm a Beatle, 'yeah, yeah!' I'm a Beatle." Unfortunately, now that I've gown up, I've become the guy with the mop on his head. "Hey, kids, look at me! Look at your Uncle Gilbert! I'm a parrot!" Of course, at that point parents frantically rush over, scoop up their children, and call the cops as I make a hasty retreat.

There were also those tiny cartoons on the margins of the pages. Those amazed me when I thought the artist drew them that tiny. When I found out he drew then normal size and they were shrunk down to tiny, I never got over it.

I always enjoyed "Spy vs. Spy." After a while, though, I did wonder why—in this day and age and with all our advanced technology—the Spies would have to resort to a giant punching glove on a spring for assassination purposes. Since then I have discovered inside information that the glove with a spring is something the CIA has had in development for several years now. They're also working on painting a large bomb like a pretty girl Spy so when you run over and kiss it, she explodes. Once again, *MAD* was ahead of its time.

Then there was the inside back cover of the magazine that you had to fold in to get the joke. Even as a kid I would look at the unfolded picture and think, "Why does that guy's shoulder look like a face and his cigarette look like a car? Still, what Al Jaffee did was always fun, like his "Snappy Answers to Stupid Questions." I always wondered why his characters couldn't just ignore the person or just hit the guy like I do to people when they ask me stupid questions. Or, for that matter, even when they *don't* ask me stupid questions, I still hit them. I just like hitting people. Hey, we all need a hobby.

I have a vague childhood recollection—it may have been in *MAD*, but I'm not positive—that there was a cartoon with a girl in her underwear and a guy saying "Gesundheit!" The gist of it, I guess, was that evidently the man had sneezed so hard he blew the girl's clothes off. (Okay, I know it was just a drawing, but it still got me excited.) To this day, whenever I sneeze, I get turned on.

"Yecch!" was a popular word with *MAD* Magazine as well. The film parodies drawn by artist Mort Drucker would always make use of it, doing things like "Titan-yecch" or "The Yecch of Living Dangerously." Although I will say it was a real thrill when Drucker did a takeoff of *Beverly Hills Cop 2*
(I don't remember what the title was, probably "Beverly Hills Cop Yecch") and he drew a picture of me as the accountant. My life had come full circle—I could finally wipe my ass with my own face. It's a neat trick, you should try it some time.

But enough about me, enjoy the book. With this new volume of the *MAD Bathroom Companion*, everyone can take *MAD* where it really belongs—in the toilet.

—Gilbert Gottfried

Gilbert Gottfried appears in three articles in this book. Find them!

How has the Soviet Union changed for Russian consumers since the fall of communism?
The Soviet Union used to be one large country with lots of shortages. Now it's eleven small countries with lots of shortages!
Why did the Russian consumer cross the road?
The lines looked shorter on the other side!
How can you tell when a National Enquirer reporter starts telling the truth?
He gets fired!
What's the best way to make disgruntled postal employee stop killing his co-workers?
Tell him it's his coffee break time!
How many disgruntled postal employees does it take to change a lightbulb?
Disgruntled postal employees don't change lightbulbs, they shoot them out with the ammo they have left over after killing ten or twenty of their former co-workers!
Why do commute train engineers hate derailments
It makes them spill their drinks!
QUIP-CHANGE ARTISTS DEPT.
NEW TW
Caroline's Comedy Club
EMO
JUDY
DRUCKER

Why did the former child TV star cross the road?
To escape police chasing him for either shoplifting, drug trafficking, or soliciting a transsexual prostitute!

Why did the euthanasia advocate cross the road?
To pull the plug on a terminally comatose patient so he could get to "the other side."

What's the difference between euthanasia and watching the Buffalo Bills in the Super Bowl?
Euthanasia is painless!

How many former child TV stars does it take to change a lightbulb?
Former child TV stars can't afford a lightbulb because their parents and managers have squandered their money!

What's the difference between euthanasia advocates and David Duke supporters?
Euthanasia advocates have no use for the braindead!

How many euthanasia advocates does it take to change a lightbulb?
One. But he changes it before it burns out, so the lightbulb can "go with dignity."

TS ON OLD JOKES

ARTIST: MORT DRUCKER WRITER: DENNIS SNEE

TEE-OLOGY DEPT.

There seems to be a new "Religion" currently attracting gre masses of followers across our land. Many sheep are strayir from the folds of Protestantism, Catholicism and Judaism t become devotees of this movement called "Dufferism" At leas

A Psalm For A

ARTIST: PAUL COKER, J

The Pro is my Shepherd;
I shall not Slice.

He maketh me to Drive Straight
down Green Fairways;

He leadeth me Safely
across Still Water-Hazards;

He restoreth my Approach Shots.

He leadeth me in the Paths of
Accuracy for my Game's Sake.

Yea, though I chip through the Roughs
in the shadows of Sand Traps,
I will fear no Bogies.

that is how it must appear to all the discouraged Ministers, Priests and Rabbis who look out over their congregations on Sabbath mornings and see so many of the men missing. And so, until these Prodigal Sons return, MAD snidely offers them:

abbath Morning

WRITER: WILLIAM GARVIN

For his Advice is with me;

His Putter and Irons,
they comfort me.

He prepareth a Strategy for me
in the presence of mine Opponents;

He anointeth my head with Confidence:
The Cup will not be runneth over!

Surely Birdies and Eagles shall follow
me all the Rounds of my Life,

And I will score in the Low Eighties—

Forever!

HANG ON, SNOOPY! DEPT.

Just as there are two sides to every war, so are there two sides to every Comic Strip. Ever since Snoopy (of "Peanuts") started telling us about his run-ins with The Red Baron, we've wondered about The Red Baron's version of this historic struggle. Well, now the story can be told! Recently,

Adventures Of

OR "Happiness Ist Ein

ARTIST: JACK RICKARD

THE RED BARON

by CARL SCHULTZ

THE RED BARON

by CARL SCHULTZ

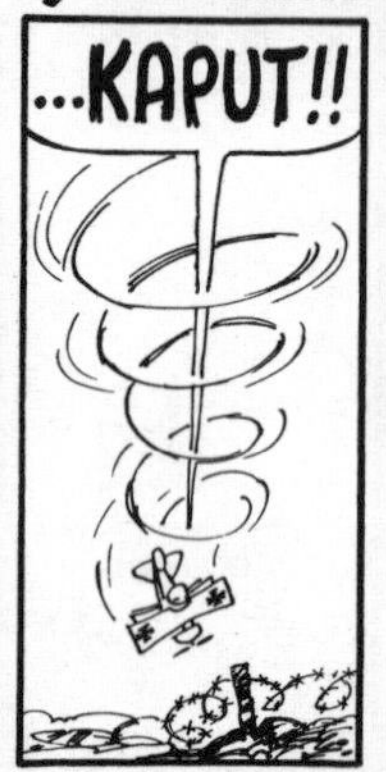

MAD's Research Staff returned from Europe with several installments of a German Comic Strip he uncovered while perusing early 1918 copies of the Hamburg Post-Dispatch. And so, for the first time in the United States, here is the other side of the story . . . mainly the hitherto unpublished . . .

The Red Baron

"Kleine Kaput Beagle"

WRITERS: FRANK JACOBS & BOB MUCCIO

THE RED BARON by CARL SCHULTZ

THE RED BARON by CARL SCHULTZ

THE RED BARON

by CARL SCHULTZ

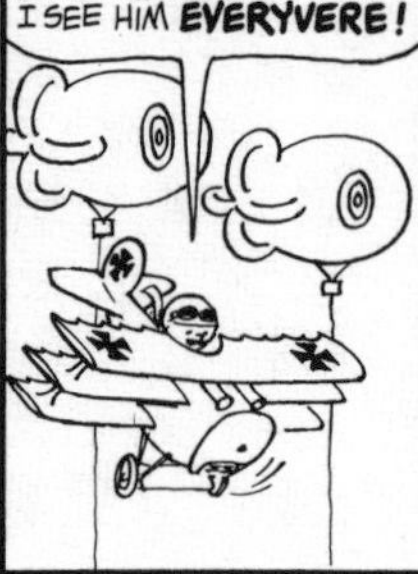

THE RED BARON

by CARL SCHULTZ

THE RED BARON

by CARL SCHULTZ

DON MARTIN DEPT.

ONE DAY ON THE BRIDGE

ANIMAL CRACK-UPS DEPT.

A PORTFOLIO OF

TURKEY

BEES

GIRAFFE

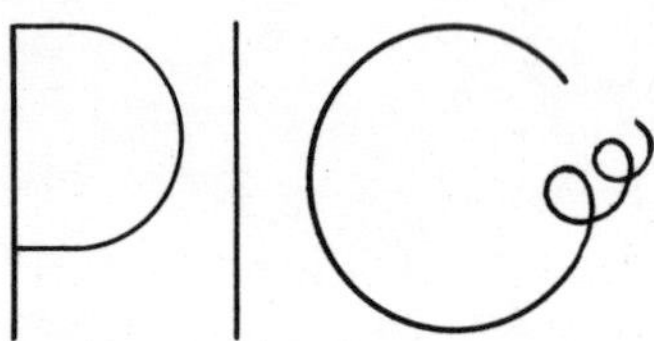

Snail

DACHSHUND

ZOO-LULUS

WRITTEN AND DESIGNED BY: MAX BRANDEL

HOOT OWL

rabbit

KANGAROO

ORM

BAT

MOUSE

COW

WOMEN LIBBERS

BERG s-EYE VIEW DEPT.

THE LIGHTE

BRAVERY

CURIOSITY

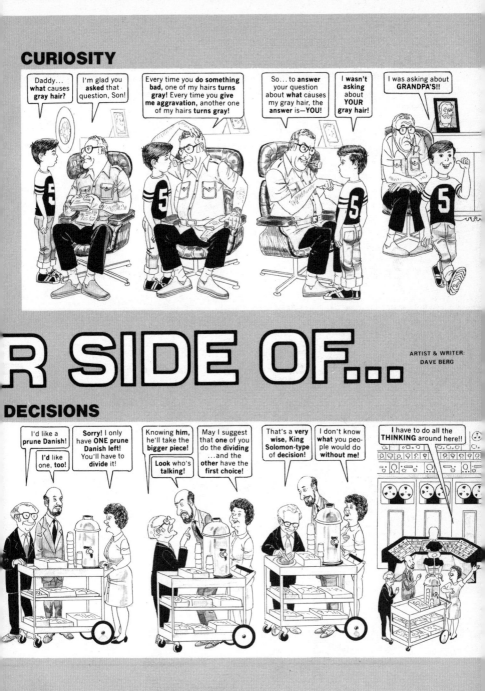

R SIDE OF...

ARTIST & WRITER:
DAVE BERG

DECISIONS

THE TELEPHONE

RELATIONSHIPS

SHOPPING

PROGRESS

GROWING UP

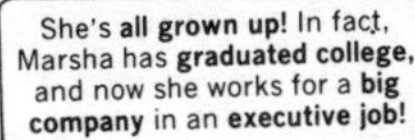

CHILDREN

VALUES

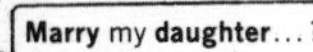

SNACKING

PARTYING

SUNDAY SCHOOL

JOKE AND DAGGER DEPT.

SPY vs SPY

CANNED LAUGHTER DEPT.

A MAD LOOK AT

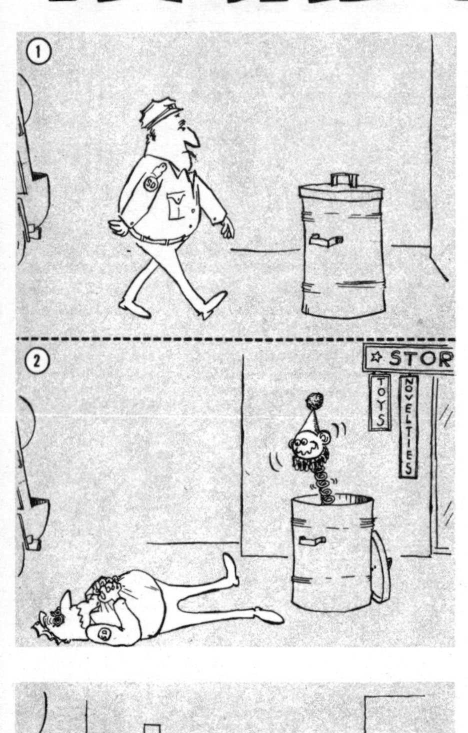

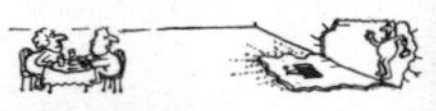

GARBAGEMEN

ARTIST & WRITER: SERGIO ARAGONES

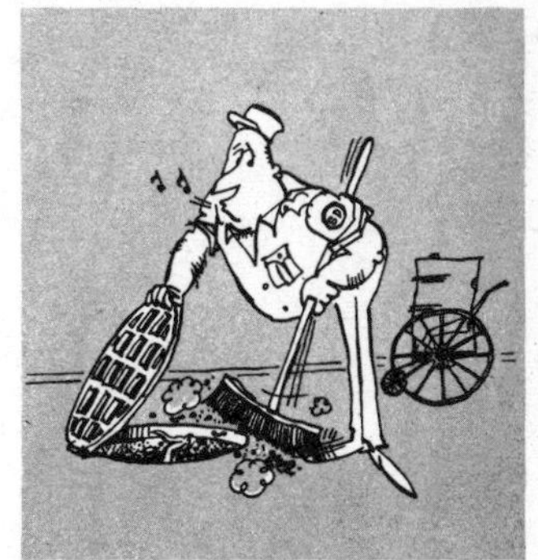

ITY DUMP
WANTED
POP ART
MUSEUM

1
GOAT FAR
2
FISH
MARKET
3
GLUE M
4
French
Perfumes
1
MAGAZINE
2
MAD MAGAZINE
850

WISE GUIDE DEPT.

MAD has come up with a device to shake up those indifferent and incompetent people you too often find yourselves at the mercy of. It's called a "Rattler". A Rattler is not something you use on the Innocent, but rather as a Defensive Weapon on people who intimidate you: the surly cab driver, the wise-guy waiter, the nasty sales clerk . . . anyone who has developed an inverted snobbery about his work and views anyone less expert as an inferior. If you run into such a person, why not try out some of these . . .

MAD R

. . . FOR SHAKING UP **WAITERS AND WAITRESSES**

No . . . I'd only like **HALF** a table! I'm not very **hungry!**

I'd like an **empty plate!** I'm on a **very strict diet!**

How about sitting down and **joining** me? Then we can **split the check,** and I won't have to leave a **tip!**

Can you bring me some **extra silverware!** I have the **same set** at home, and I'm **missing** a few pieces!

I'll have the **same** thing that I ordered yesterday! I **didn't TOUCH it** yesterday!

I'll have the **steak dinner** . . . with no potatoes . . . no vegetables . . . and no **meat!**

The **menu** looks **good!** I'll eat **THAT!**

I'm very **intimidated** by **Waiters!** So may I **start tipping** you **NOW?**

Miss, would you be **offended** if I **sent out** for some **food?**

My compliments to the **Chef** . . . for having **the nerve** to pass **this stuff off** as **food!**

Hey, this food isn't **half bad** . . . it's **ALL bad!**

Waiter, give me a **very small check!** I'm in a **hurry!**

. . . FOR SHAKING UP **BARBERS**

I **know** it's my turn, but I just can't stop reading these **three-year-old magazines!**
Before you touch my hair, can you show me **proof** that you're **Italian?**
I'd like it **longer** in the **back,** . . . and **thicker** on **top,** please!
Never mind the **haircut!** Just tell me your idictic **opinions!**
Tell me, do you **shave legs?**

. . . FOR SHAKING UP **TELEPHONE OPERATORS**

Operator, I put a **dime** in and got back **ten dollars in quarters!** If you tell me your **address,** I'll **send** it to you in **stamps!**
Operator, I'd like to make a **long distance call!** How far from the phone do **I stand?**
Operator, what do you have that's **exciting** in **3-message-unit calls?**
Operator, may I have a **wrong number?** This is an **emergency!**
Information . . .? Are you really a beautiful blonde?

ATTLERS

ARTIST: JACK DAVIS WRITER: LARRY GORE

...FOR SHAKING UP **SALES HELP**

Does this come with **two pair of pants?** The **TIE,** I mean!

Do you have anything that's marked down to **"FREE"?**

I'd like to see something **terribly overpriced!**

I'd like to get this **exact same suit** ... but in a **completely different style!**

I need a **complete new wardrobe!** Can you recommend a **good store?**

Do you have something **much too large** for me! **I love alterations!**

How soon can I **return** this?

May I **charge** this ... to **YOU?**

ROBERT STALL

MAY I HELP YOU

...FOR SHAKING UP **ELEVATOR OPERATORS**

To the **Penthouse,** driver ... and **don't stop** for any **lights!**
Do you get **extra pay** for flying **dangerous missions?**
How could they send a **kid** up in a crate like **this?**
Twice around the **building,** driver! We're in **love!**
Would the **4th floor** take you out of your way?
Here's a buck! Take me to **another building!**
Uh ... where's the **Men's Room** in this car? I think I'm going to be **sick ...**

...FOR SHAKING UP **CAB DRIVERS**

I'm from **out of town!** How about a **tour** of your **famous slums?**
Driver, drop me off at the **nearest cab!** I'm in a **hurry!**
Is it true that in this State, **tipping** is **illegal?**
That's the **second** pedestrian you **MISSED!** Are you **sure** you haven't been **DRINKING?**
Stop the cab! That's **not your picture!**
Drive slowly! I'm looking for a **date!**
Would you mind turning off the meter? The **ticking** gives me a **headache!**
Where's the **Men's Room** in this cab? I think I'm going to be **sick ...**
$2.33

COMES THE YAWN DEPT.

You Know You're REA

You Know You're REALLY A BORE When . . .

. . . you're at the beach, and your date buries himself in the sand . . . completely.

You Know You're REALLY A BORE When . . .

. . . a letter you wrote home to your Mother is returned unopened with the notation: "Nobody here by that name!" . . . and the notation is in your Mother's handwriting.

You Know You're REALLY A BORE When . . .

. . . obscene phone-callers hang up on *you*.

You Know You're REALLY A BORE When . . .

. . . you're in Confession, and your Priest interrupts you to ask: "What's a 3-letter word for a European Blackbird?"

You Know You're REALLY A BORE When . . .

. . . people at parties always seem to mistake you for a hypnotist.

You Know You're REALLY A BORE When . . .

. . . even the Avon Lady won't call on you.

You Know You're REALLY A BORE When . . .

. . . your psychiatrist has "Let's Make A Deal" on his TV set during your sessions.

You Know You're REALLY A BORE When . . .

. . . you overhear the F.B.I. man who's tapping your phone humming to himself

.LY A BORE When...

ARTIST:
PAUL COKER, JR.

WRITER:
STAN HART

u Know You're REALLY A BORE When . . .

. your friend cuts your visit short by saying, "I've t a million things to do!" . . . and he's in traction.

You Know You're REALLY A BORE When . . .

. . . your dentist makes you keep the cotton swabs in your mouth until you're out of his office.

You Know You're REALLY A BORE When . . .

. . . your guests *ask* to see your home movies.

ou Know You're EALLY A BORE When . . .

. your teacher thanks you for answering question before you finish answering it.

You Know You're REALLY A BORE When . . .

. . . the barber puts a hot towel over your face, and you're only getting a haircut.

You Know You're REALLY A BORE When . . .

. . . a girl breaks a date with you in order to go to a Montreal Expos-San Diego Padres double-header.

You Know You're REALLY A BORE When . . .

. . . the little old lady you've helped half-way across the street runs the rest of the way herself.

You Know You're REALLY A BORE When . . .

. . . your whole life suddenly flashes before your eyes, and it doesn't even hold your interest.

DON MARTIN DEPT.

A QUICK STROLL

URBAN ON THE ROCKS DEPT.

It doesn't take a genius to see that our cities are in big trouble these days. Mass Transit is in a shambles, streets are caving in around us, and employee productivity is down. Take a look at this typical city to see what we mean...

ARTIST: HARRY NORTH   WRITER: DICK DE BARTOLO AND FRED BLOCK

Now for the really bad news. When you turn this page, you're going to see some of the dumbest ideas, proposals and solutions ever conceived in an article called

MAD'S SUGGESTIONS FOR HOW OUR CITIES CAN SOLVE THEIR PROBLEMS

(While Clearing A Little Extra Cash On The Side!)

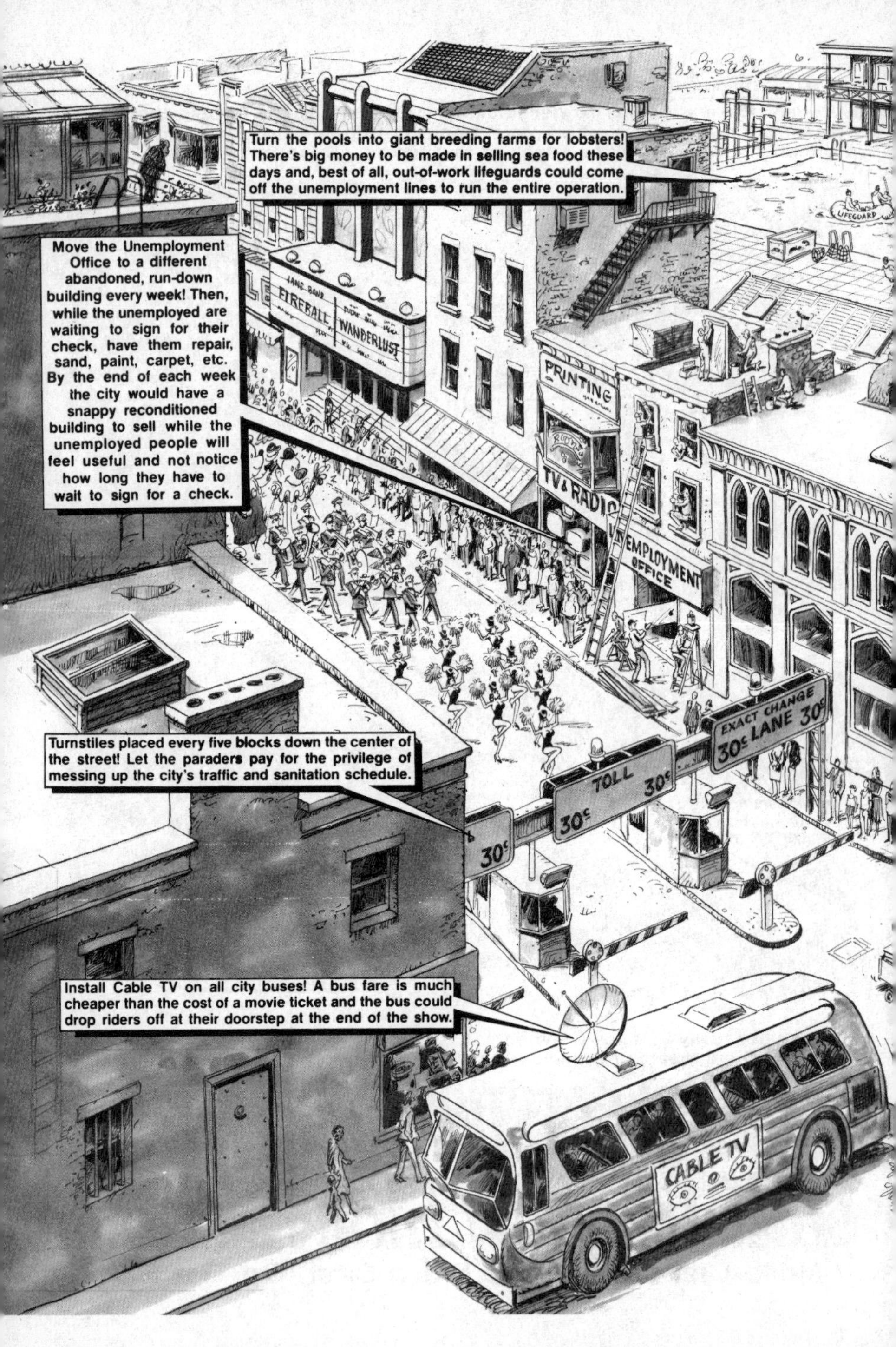
Turn the pools into giant breeding farms for lobsters! There's big money to be made in selling sea food these days and, best of all, out-of-work lifeguards could come off the unemployment lines to run the entire operation.
LIFEGUARD
Move the Unemployment Office to a different abandoned, run-down building every week! Then, while the unemployed are waiting to sign for their check, have them repair, sand, paint, carpet, etc. By the end of each week the city would have a snappy reconditioned building to sell while the unemployed people will feel useful and not notice how long they have to wait to sign for a check.
FIREBALL
WANDERLUST
PRINTING
TV & RADIO
UNEMPLOYMENT OFFICE
Turnstiles placed every five blocks down the center of the street! Let the paraders pay for the privilege of messing up the city's traffic and sanitation schedule.
EXACT CHANGE
30¢ LANE 30¢
TOLL
30¢
30¢
30¢
Install Cable TV on all city buses! A bus fare is much cheaper than the cost of a movie ticket and the bus could drop riders off at their doorstep at the end of the show.
CABLE TV

Carling's
FOR LEASE
BAR
Quinns
FIRE DEPARTMENT
First National Bank
BURGERS
OPEN
POLICE
Put the firemen to work during slack time periods as window washers for high-rise office and apart ment buildings. The city and firemen could split whatever they make 50-50.
Forget spending millions to repave, get celebrities to sign the potholes! If schmucks travel from all over to see star's foot prints on Hollywood Blvd., you can bet they'll flock to see your local "Celebrity Potholes!"
Double Parking Meters! Sure, double parking is illegal, but as long as motorists are going to do it anyway, they might as well be forced to pay double the normal rates.
Load up police car trunks with letters, parcels, pizzas —anything that needs quick, same-day delivery service. Since police have to drive through neighborhoods anyway, and have the extra advantage of being able to use their siren, they'll be able to give cheaper and faster service than any local messenger service while turning big, big profits for both themselves and the city's empty coffers.
SNAP?
SNAP!

NEW LEASH ON LIFE DEPT.

A MAD LOOK AT...

OBEDIENCE TRA

Since an unruly dog can be a pest, and a well-trained dog can be a wonderful companion, the "Obedience School For Dogs" has become very popular lately. However, the same can be said for kids! Since an unruly child can be a pest, and a well-trained child can be a joy . . .

WHY NOT "OBEDIENCE SCHO

AND WHY NOT "OBEDIENCE SCHOOLS FOR HUSBANDS"?

NING

ARTIST & WRITER: DEAN NORMAN

OLS FOR KIDS"?

Wouldn't it be great if we could train kids to obey a few simple commands, such as . . .

AND WHY NOT "OBEDIENCE SCHOOLS FOR WIVES"?!?

"X" PLOY-TATION DEPT.

Take a look at the ads for movies, and you can sure tell what sells films these days: Sex! Nudity! Drugs! Wild living! That's what brings the crowds to theatres! Well, this may work for the free-wheeling flicks of today . . . but what about the revivals of all those "square," mild movies of yesterday?

ADS FOR MO

ARTIST: BOB CLARKE

How do you advertise a re-release of something like . . . say . . . "Snow White and the Seven Dwarfs" or "Born Free" to modern movie audiences? The answer, my friends, is written in these ads . . . the answer is written in these ads. So follow their example, and stretch the truth, like we've done with these

VIE REVIVALS

WRITER: FRANK JACOBS

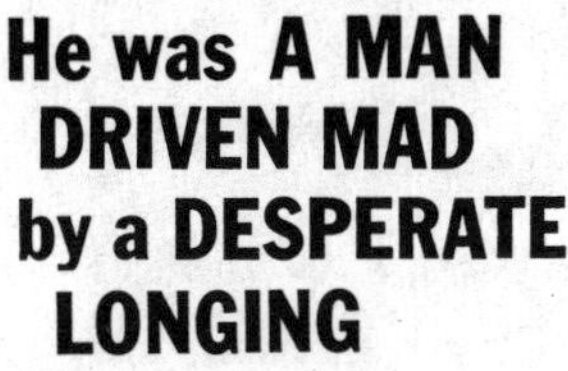

To touch—
To fondle—
To possess

THE FORBIDDEN FLESH THAT TORMENTED HIS DESIRE!

A Man of the World Consumed by Waves of Passion! He had All He Desired—EXCEPT The One He Desired Most of All!

MOBY—

A Shimmering Creature of Abnormal Appetites Whose Soft, Curved, White, Tantalizing Body was TOO WILD Ever to be Possessed!

A RAW, NAKED STORY— PULSATING WITH PASSION!

MOBY DICK

"Goes to great depths . . . a whale of a climax!"—De Generate, STAR

THEY "DROPPED OUT" OF LIFE ON A 40-YEAR FREAK-OUT IN THE DESERT!
They were the Now generation of 1200 B.C.—a far-out cult of Flower Children who thumbed their noises at the establishment until one cat with long hair, beard and sandals offered them "Tablets" that turned them all on! Where did he get them? Out of sight, man!
SEE MIND-BLOWING SCENES IN PSYCHEDELIC COLOR!
Pax
See the Red Sea split, then return to "zap" the Pharaoh's Pig Army!!
See Moses rap with God on Mount Sinai
GROOVE ON
"THE TEN COMMANDMENTS"
"The bad trip with the Golden Calf flipped my wig!" Moss, ROLLING STONE

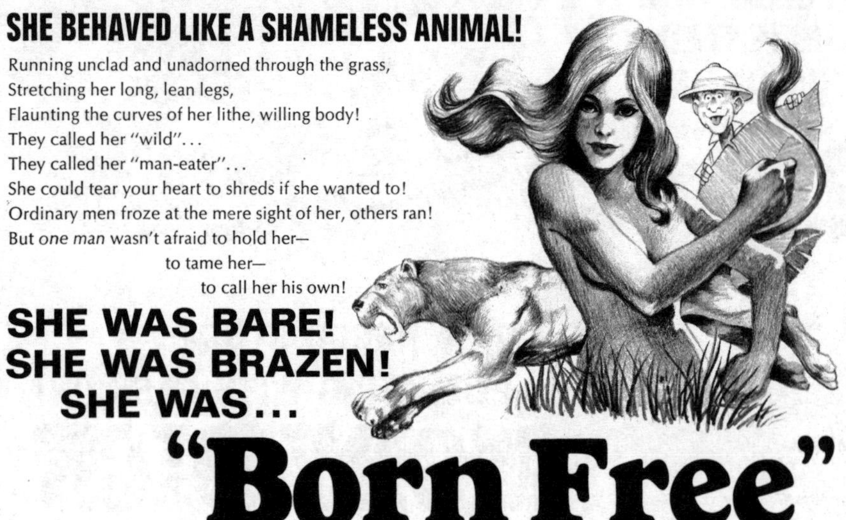
SHE BEHAVED LIKE A SHAMELESS ANIMAL!
Running unclad and unadorned through the grass,
Stretching her long, lean legs,
Flaunting the curves of her lithe, willing body!
They called her "wild"...
They called her "man-eater"...
She could tear your heart to shreds if she wanted to!
Ordinary men froze at the mere sight of her, others ran!
But one man wasn't afraid to hold her—
to tame her—
to call her his own!
SHE WAS BARE!
SHE WAS BRAZEN!
SHE WAS...
"Born Free"
"She has a lot to show, and she seems to like showing it!"—Oggle, PLAYBOY

ZODIACS MURDER DEPT.

YOUR MAD HOROSCOPE

TODAY'S BIRTHDAY:

Your birthday was last month, schmuck! Ask your mother for the *full* story!

ARIES
March 21—April 19

Dramatic developments! Some strong astrological forces clash—leaving your Moon Over Miami. Don't worry! This is not a Blue Moon, so you will bask in a magnificent Moonglow as Moonlight Becomes You. If any part of this horoscope confuses you, consult one of your parents or a friendly cocktail-hour piano player.

TAURUS
April 20—May 20

Romantic entanglements can pose some problems so lay off the S&M for awhile. Focus on career matters, making sure your finger is not in front of the lens. The PM is an excellent time for love, so make sure you have an extra $50 tucked in your wallet should the opportunity arise. (Put the rest of your cash in your shoe.)

GEMINI
May 21—June 21

The Big Dipper and the Little Dipper are jointly sending you messages. They're doing this to cut down on postage and handling charges which, as you know, are astronomical. The stars warn you that things at home are not what they appear. Beware especially of a Colonial-style sofa, a five speed blender or a bearded child.

MOON CHILDREN
June 22—July 22

A funny day. A washed-up comic in the Catskills is planning a big comeback at your expense. His words carry great weight, as does your blind date this evening. A small change in personnel where you work greatly improves conditions for everyone involved. In other words, you're getting the ax sometime this morning.

LEO
July 23—August 22

Your stars point to a new cycle and it's a beauty!—a bright red 10-speeder! Unfortunately, one of the foot pedals is missing, as are the screws for the hand brakes. Until these parts are ordered, it's back to riding the bus. Take heart! Make the most of your current success. Incredible as it may seem, you've peaked.

VIRGO
August 23—September 22

A troubling day. A piece of poultry is not as dead as you think, and is just waiting for you to open that refrigerator door. A business deal may take you out of town, but only a blind idiot would take you out to dinner! You refuse to think about anything but "the present". Buy him a shirt, and get it over with!

LIBRA
September 23—October 23

Financial strains preoccupy you, but it's the neglected physical strain that could leave you with a hideous limp. Thoroughly test a new love before falling for him or her head-over-heels. (Use either a True-or-False or Multiple Choice format. Essay questions never work right and will take you much longer to grade.)

SCORPIO
October 24—November 21

As you enter a new cycle, the stars are promising you an intense romance with a Leo. Normally, you would be compatable. In this case, however, the stars are referring to Leo Flogs—the town drunk and a suspected carrier of malaria and mail. Your idea spells profit. What is unknown is how do you spell relief?

SAGITTARIUS
November 22—December 21

Your moon is in the House of Representatives, where undercover FBI men are secretly filming its acceptance of a bribe. You have private wishes and opinions that are best left unvoiced as they are disgusting and depraved. A surprise promotion comes when a co-worker takes a leave of absence to give birth to your child.

CAPRICORN
December 22—January 19

Personal sacrifices for a child will bring you instant fame and financial gains. Then again, so probably would your sacrificing *of* a child! Appealing offers are not what they seem, so be prepared for a letdown when a current love finally lets you put your hand in her blouse. A horrible disease arises at school.

AQUARIUS
January 20—February 18

Some astral forces are playing tug-of-war with you now, so next time you buy a shirt, be sure to get a longer sleeve length. Work while others play, and you will grab the brass ring. You can either wear it on your pinky, or sell it for scrap. Cut through red tape. However, please do not fold, spindle or mutilate it.

PISCES
February 19—March 20

An indecisive attitude on the part of someone you rely on for advice could get you into real trouble. Then again, it may not. Work keeps you from family affairs and family affairs keep you from work. Just what exactly you do all day remains one of life's great unsolved mysteries.

WRITER: JOHN FICARRA

MISFORTUNE KOOKIE DEPT.

It always happens! You plot and you plan and you work to carve out a perfect little life for yourself. But no matter how carefully you look before you leap, and save

Don't You Feel L

DON'T YOU FEEL LIKE A SCHMUCK...
... preparing for winter with the best snow tires money can buy... ... and winding up stuck behind a guy who didn't!

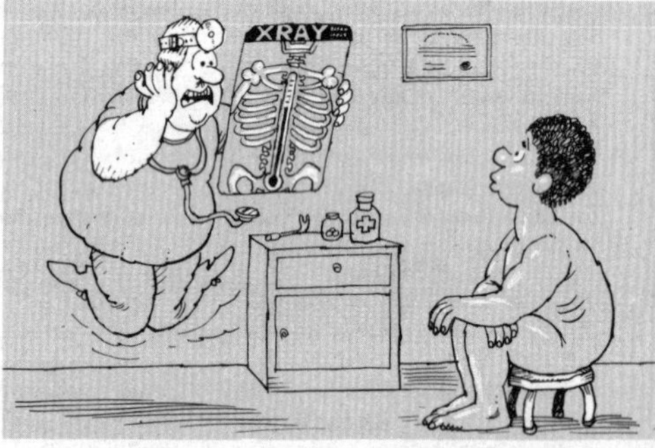

DON'T YOU FEEL LIKE A SCHMUCK...
... eating fish to cut down on cholesterol... ... and accumulating enough mercury in your system to kill a whale!

DON'T YOU FEEL LIKE A SCHMUCK...
... putting on an expensive exotic perfume... ... and the person you're spending the evening with smells like a goat!

for a rainy day, some event—completely beyond your control—brings the whole scheme tumbling down. And as you sit there in the rubble and ruin of your best-laid plans—

ke A Schmuck?!

ARTIST & WRITER: AL JAFFEE

DON'T YOU FEEL LIKE A SCHMUCK...
...obeying your County's anti-pollution laws...

...when your water comes from another County with no such laws!

DON'T YOU FEEL LIKE A SCHMUCK...
...getting to the theater early to get a good seat...

...and at the last minute, an eight-foot giant picks the only empty seat left... the one directly in front of you!

DON'T YOU FEEL LIKE A SCHMUCK...
...doing all you can do to avoid catching a cold...

...and some careless, sick slob coughs right in your face!

DON'T YOU FEEL LIKE A SCHMUCK . . .
. . . paying a fortune to fly in order to save time . . . . . . and spending the time you save in an airport traffic jam!

DON'T YOU FEEL LIKE A SCHMUCK . . .
. . . spending months, training your dog to "go" in one special out-of-the-way spot . . . . . . while your neighbor lets his dog loose to "go" wherever it pleases!

DON'T YOU FEEL LIKE A SCHMUCK . . .
. . . taking perfect care of your teeth for thirty-three years . . . . . . and blowing it all on one stupid barroom argument!

DON'T YOU FEEL LIKE A SCHMUCK . . .
. . . compressing your garbage into neat little packs . . . . . . and the neighbors' loose stuff ends up all over your lawn!

DON'T YOU FEEL LIKE A SCHMUCK . . .
. . . making sure you're insured to the hilt . . .

. . . and your *un*insured Mother-in-Law's 14-month illness wipes you out!

DON'T YOU FEEL LIKE A SCHMUCK . . .
. . . coaching, advising and helping your fellow worker for years, because he's sending his son through college . . .

. . . and the kid finally graduates . . . right into your job!

DON'T YOU FEEL LIKE A SCHMUCK . . .
. . . moving to the country to escape the sounds of the city . . .

. . . without first checking out the sounds of the country!

DON'T YOU FEEL LIKE A SCHMUCK . . .
. . . buying a new garment with a special washing instruction label sewn right into the lining . . .

. . . and the first moron who launders it completely ignores the label!

FAT'S ENTERTAINMENT DEPT.

LOOK SLIM AND T DIET OR STRENU

MINGLE WITH PEOPLE THAT ARE FATTER THAN YOU ARE

WEAR CLOTHES THAT ARE TWO SIZES TOO BIG

CAREFULLY CHOOSE EMPLOYMENT THAT WILL HIDE YOUR GIRTH

USE CORNERS AND ENTRANCES TO REDUCE YOUR APPEARANCE

PROPER HAIR AND BEARD STYLE CAN GIVE YOUR FACE THAT LEAN AND HUNGRY LOOK

RIM WITHOUT US EXERCISE

A MAD "HOW TO DO IT" FEATURE

ARTIST AND WRITER: PAUL PETER PORGES

TRY TO EMPHASIZE YOUR OUTSTANDING FEATURES

ALWAYS SELECT OVERSTUFFED FURNITURE TO SIT IN

MAKE CLEVER USE OF HOUSE PLANTS TO YOUR ADVANTAGE

WEAR DARK CLOTHING...AND THEN TRY TO STAND AGAINST DARK SHADOWY BACKGROUNDS

ALWAYS DATE PEOPLE THAT ARE EVEN FATTER THAN YOU

PUTTING "HAH" ON YOUR CHEST DEPT.

One of the most popular fashion phenomena among young people these days is th T-shirt with a message. You've seen them (and probably wear them). They've go messages like "Property of Alcatraz," "Kiss Me, I'm Italian," "My Folks Visite

T-SHIRTS WITH MESS

as Vegas And All I Got Was This Lousy T-Shirt," and so on. Well, we think that stead of sporting clever but rather impersonal machine-made comments, people ould reveal their true thoughts about themselves and their shirts with these

GES WE'D LIKE TO SEE

ARTIST: GEORGE WOODBRIDGE WRITER: LARRY SIEGEL

PUNISHMENTAL IMAGES DEPT.

WISHFUL

NOISE MAKERS

TELEPHONE BOOTH HOGS

ARTIST: HARRY NORTH

PARTY SMART-ALECS

NOSE-IN-THE-AIR SNOBS

SMOKE POLLUTERS

UMBRELLA SHAKERS

THINKING

WRITER: PAUL PETER PORGES

MESSY EATERS

SLOBBERING AUNTS

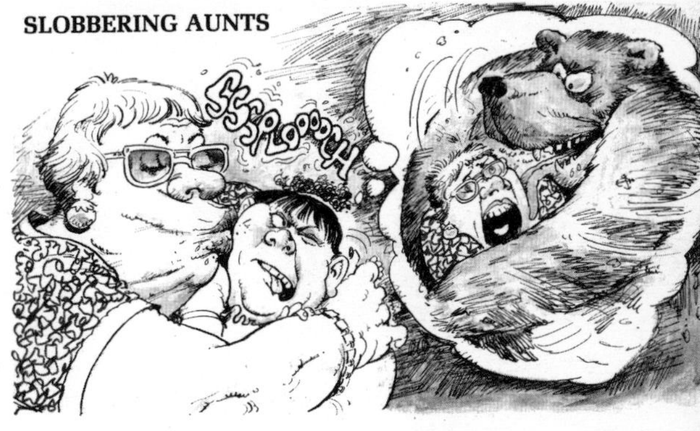

PARK MASHERS

CENTERLINE DRIVERS

NASTY DOGS

MOTORCYCLE BULLIES

SMELLY ROOM MATES

DON MARTIN DEPT.

ONE EVENING AT HOME

ROAM, SWEET HOME DEPT.

The Mobile Home craze is sweeping the world. But the trouble is, Mobile Homes

CUSTOMIZED M

...THAT REFLECT WHERE

ARTIST & WRITER:

l look pretty much alike. They lack ethnic character. So why not design...

OBILE HOMES

HEIR OWNERS ARE FROM

UL COKER, JR.

WESTERN OZ

ESTERN U.S.A.

THE VATICAN

JAPAN

INDIA

NEVADA

HOME SWEET MOBILE HOME

HEAVEN SENT DEPT.

**Recently, someone published a book called "Children's Letters To Go
It was so popular, another book was published called "More Childre
Letters To God." Now, that one is so popular, by the time you read t**

Answers To Childre

WRITERS: DICK DeBARTOLO & DONALD K. EPSTEIN

Dear Bruce,
I am sorry it rained last Sunday when you were supposed to have your Boy Scout Hike, but I cannot send you a copy of my "Guaranteed Long-Range Forecast" to avoid disappointments like that in the future.
Faithfully yours,
God

Dear Lisa,
Your forthcoming trip to California sounds very exciting. I would love to see you, too, but TWA does not stop here on the way to Los Angeles.
Fondly,
God

Dear Tommy,
The reason you cannot find me in the telephone book is that my number is unlisted.
Best wishes,
God

Dear Mary,
My notes about your behavior are written in the Big Book in indelible ink. But thank you anyway for the nice eraser.
Love,
God

Dear Beth,
I am sorry, but it is not up to me to make bacon "kosher."
Sincerely,
God

Dear Laurie,
Yes, I am watching you all the time. But that is no excuse for not taking a bath.
Love,
God

Dear Jerry,
I do spend a lot of time in Brooklyn, but that was not Me you saw on the IND subway last Saturday afternoon.
Love,
God

Dear Sharon,
I was very pleased to learn that you think of your good deeds as "deposits in the Bank of Life." However, I do not have the facilities for sending you a regular monthly statement.
Best regards,
God

icle, they'll probably publish one called "Still More Children's tters To God." Well, it seems to us that there's an awful lot of e-way letter-writing going on, so MAD remedies the situation with

Letters–From GOD

PHOTO BY D.P.I.

Dear Linda,
I am glad you received a new camera for your birthday, but it would be against the rules to let you come up here and take pictures.
Love,
God

Dear Jonathan,
Thanks for your inquiry, but I really do not have a favorite. I like all the Commandments.
Love,
God

Dear Leslie,
Thank you for your concern, but I do not find it a "drag" working Sundays and religious holidays.
Sincerely,
God

Dear Susie,
I know you have doubts about my existence, but in the future please do not address your letters to:
Occupant,
Heaven,
U.S.A.
Thank you.
Sincerely,
God

Dear Robin,
Even though your daddy says they are "God-awful," I am not responsible for the shows you watch on television.
Sincerely,
God

Dear Tracy,
You may tell your mommy I said it is not a "sin" to leave the peas in your TV dinner.
Love,
God

Dear Edward,
You sound like a very enterprising young man, but I really do not feel that there is a market for holy water in "No-deposit, No-return Bottles."
Sincerely,
God

Dear Randy and Ricky,
It does not matter which one of you sleeps where. I'm just as close to the one in the bottom bunk.
Love,
God

Dear Harvey,
Yes, I can hear you singing in the church choir every Sunday.

Do not call Us --
We will call you.
Sincerely,
God

MAD SALUTES THE OUTPUT OF AMERICAN INDUSTRY

CONCEIVED BY MAX BRANDEL

RINGSNIDE SEAT DEPT.

Pro Football is slipping in popularity because the guys in charge have decided to cut down on the violence. They've even made it illegal to dance after creaming an opponent. And our other violent sport, Hockey, is also cleaning up its act. It's cutting down on fighting, and a player can be suspended just for conking somebody with his stick. So fans have been looking elsewhere for their sports entertainment, and they are turning in increasing numbers to that old standby, Wrestling...which is our excuse for presenting another of our ridiculous Primers.

THE MAD WRESTLING PRIMER

ARTIST: JACK DAVIS WRITER: LOU SILVERSTONE

Chapter One

See the people standing on line.
It is a long, long, long line.
There are Doctors and Lawyers on line.
There are Artists and Writers on line.
There are Teachers and Brokers on line.
They are waiting to buy tickets to a Wrestling Match.
Do they enjoy Wrestling because they like violence and bloodshed?
No...they claim they like to watch Wrestling for the laughs.
They also claim they like to read "Playboy" for the interviews.

Chapter Two

See the man.
He weighs over three hundred pounds.
He looks like he escaped from the zoo.
When he enters the ring, he hits the Referee,
He curses the Announcer,
He spits at the Crowd.
Is this ugly slob a Wrestler?
No, he is only a Manager...
If he is only a Manager...
Can you imagine what his Wrestler is like?

Chapter Three

See the man in the striped shirt.
He is the Referee.
His job is to control the Wrestlers,
And to see that they obey the rules.
The Referee weighs 97 pounds.
Each Wrestler weighs over 250 pounds.
How do they expect a 97 pound man
To control over 500 pounds of angry Wrestlers?
They don't.
It wouldn't be any fun if he could.
Which is why Wrestling is such a popular sport.

Chapter Four

See the terrifying man.
He is a Wrestler.
He is "The Wild Man From Borneo."
He bites the ropes.
He bites the microphone.
He bites the Referee.
What does he do to his opponent?
Don't ask.
His Manager claims he found him in the jungles of Borneo.
He really found him working in a "7-11 Store" on Staten Island.
Why do they call him "The Wild Man From Borneo"?
Would you pay $12 to see "The Grocery Bagger From Staten Island"?

Chapter Five

See the Wrestlers.
The one on the left is an American Indian.
His name is "Chief Bloody Scalp."
His favorite hold is "The Tomahawk Decapitator."
Next to him is "Captain U.S."
His favorite hold is "The Red, White & Blue Eyeball-Gouger."
Next to him is "The Polish Assassin."
His favorite hold is "The Warsaw Light Bulb Twister."

Now see the last Wrestler on the right.
He doesn't have a fancy name.
He doesn't have a flashy costume.
He doesn't even have a gimmicky hold.
He's just an expert in Scientific Wrestling.
This guy is never going to make it
As a Professional Wrestler.
Even if he was the National Amateur Champion.

Chapter Six

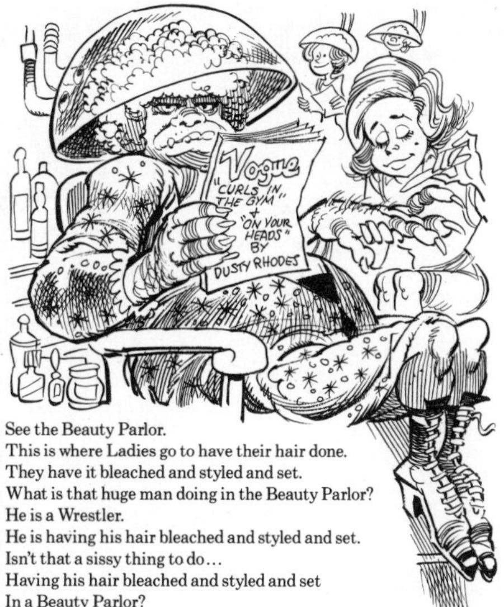

See the Beauty Parlor.
This is where Ladies go to have their hair done.
They have it bleached and styled and set.
What is that huge man doing in the Beauty Parlor?
He is a Wrestler.
He is having his hair bleached and styled and set.
Isn't that a sissy thing to do…
Having his hair bleached and styled and set
In a Beauty Parlor?
Sure…!
But YOU tell him!

Chapter Seven

See the Wrestlers holding up their belts.
Those are Championship Belts.
Does that mean they are all Champions.
Absolutely.
One is the AWA Champ; one is the SWA Champ;
One is the SWT Champ; one is the WC Champ;
One is the WWT Champ and one is the WWA Champ.
Wrestling is the only sport
Where there are more Champions than Challengers.

Chapter Eight

See the Wrestlers on TV
They look like two fat slobs.
But the Announcer says they're in great shape.
They aren't doing anything but falling on top of each other.
But the Announcer makes their match sound like World War III.
Is there something wrong with the Announcer's eyes?
No… he can see very well.
He can see himself on the Unemployment Line
If he tells it like it is.

Chapter Nine

See the angry Wrestling Fans.
They take their Wrestling very seriously.
They believe that everything that happens
In the Wrestling Ring is for real.
See them beating up on a Spectator.
Punch, punch, kick, kick.
Why are they beating up on this poor man?
Because he said that Wrestling is a phony.
And this makes Wrestling Fans very angry.
P.T. Barnum would have loved Wrestling.
Because he said "There's a sucker born every minute."
Too bad the angry Wrestling Fans can't see
That the Spectator they're beating up on
Is the only one who's really getting hurt in the Arena tonight.

INSIDE-OUCH DEPT.

Okay, gang, here we go again with another visit behind the scenes of an American institution

A MAD PEEK BEHIND

discover what new and inventive ways we the people are being shafted. Won't you join us for

THE SCENES AT A SHOPPING CENTER

ARTIST: BOB CLARKE WRITER: STAN HART

I see you're showing an **"X-Rated"** novie! Which one is it?

Walt Disney's **"101 Dalmatians"**!

I don't understand!

We gotta do **SOMETHING** to get the kids in!!

RAW UNCUT VERSION! RATED "X"

NOW SHOWING

EVEN THE TITLE IS RATED X

FIX BY SEPT

We **used** to have offices on the 20th, 21st and 22nd floors of a building **downtown**!

Oh? And you like it better being in the **suburbs**—all under **one roof?**

Not really! It's just that now—when those **market crashes** occur—no one gets hurt jumping out of **our windows!!**

PETERS, PIPER, PICHEL & PECK STOCK BROKERS

AUTO SEAT C

Mr. Stanley

DRIVE-IN BANK

There's absolutely **no shade** in this lot, and those **door handles** can get hot enough to give you a **third degree burn!** Isn't that **awful?**

Are you **kidding?** It's **GREAT!**

What are you . . . a **sadist?!**

No . . . a **Druggist!!**

But I thought you'd be **happy** that I got you a sponsor for your Little League Team!

Did you have to get **THAT** sponsor?

I don't understand!

You think it's **fun** for a kid to be a member of **"Mr. Stanley's House Of Beauty Yankees"?!**

Now, when you're giving **bills**, you have to wait for the **wind** out there!

Er—until it **dies down?**

No, until it **starts up!** You should see the money **fly!** It's a **laugh-riot!**

But—how about **silver?**

Oh, **that** you just drop a few inches short of the **car** so it falls to the **ground!**

DRIVE-IN BANK

IN

OUT

AMERICAN

n just 6 short weeks, e **firmed up** her arms nd legs, **lost** her flab, ned up her muscles—and now she looks like an **old BULL!**

GYM

You mean I can bring my dress in at **Noon**, and get it out at **1 P.M.?!** How do you **do** it?

How long does it take to **press it**, staple a **tag** on it, and put it in a **plastic bag?!**

But, don't you **CLEAN** it?

Show me where it says anything about **cleaning!**

ONE HOUR SERVICE

I can fix **ALMOST anything!** But **HER**, you better take to a **plastic surgeon!**

I'm not **talking** about her! I'm talking about **her wrist watch!**

FIX IT SHOP

THINGS MADE GOOD AS NEW AGAIN

SLEEPER PLAY DEPT.

The Psycholo

THE NORMAL PERSON

THE PATRIOT

THE EXTROVERT

THE EGOTIST

The Escapist

The Neurotic

The Psychotic

THE SADIST

THE MASOCHIST

gy Of Snoring

WRITER: FRANK JACOBS

THE INTROVERT

The Non-Conformist

THE INHIBITED

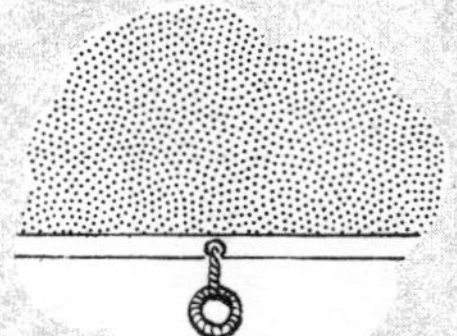

the mystic

The Amnesiac

THE ALCOHOLIC

The Inferiority Complex

The Persecution Complex

The Insomniac

SCHOOL

Class, my name is Miss Green, and I'm a Teacher-In-Training! I'd like to get to know something about all of you! Let's start with what you would all like to be when you grow up!

I'd like to be an Astronaut!
I'd like to be a Doctor!
I'd like to be a Nurse!
I'd like to be a Lawyer!

I'd like to be just like YOU, Miss Green!
You mean a Teacher-In-Training??

BERG'S-EYE VIEW DEPT.

THE LIGHTE

BLAME

Hey, Mom!! Donald broke your favorite potted plant!!
I DID NOT! You did!

No, YOU did!!
You're a LIAR! YOU did!!

Okay... knock it off! Just calm down and tell me exactly what happened!
It was Donald's fault!! All I was doing was holding the potted plant...

And then, when I threw it at him, he DUCKED!!

BUSINESS

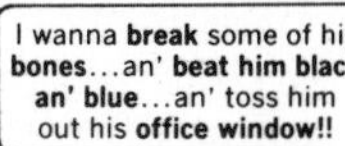

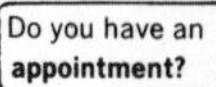

ARTIST & WRITER:
DAVE BERG

WEDDINGS

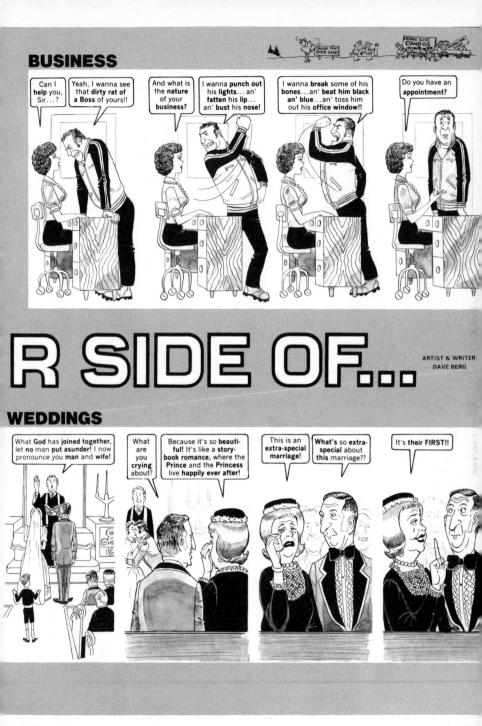

INVITATIONS

POWER

ETIQUETTE

MODERN EDUCATION

THE FUTURE

COLLEGE

EXPERIMENTS

Sure! With the **price** of **gold** so **high** these days, you'd **never** do anything **that dumb!**

CHORES

MAKING OUT

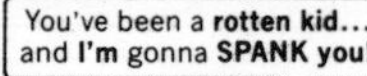

PUNISHMENT

DON MARTIN DEPT.

At The Academy Of Electric Fan Repair

FOR REPEAT'S SAKE! DEPT.

INSTANT TV REPL

KARPOV'S MOVE OF KNIGHT'S PAWN FROM Q-6 TO Q-7

DOUBLE FOUL COMMITTED DURING N.I.T. TOURNAMENT

UMPIRE'S CHECK OF WEATHER DURING RAIN DELAY

EXCITED CONTESTANT'S LEAP ON "THE PRICE IS RIGHT"

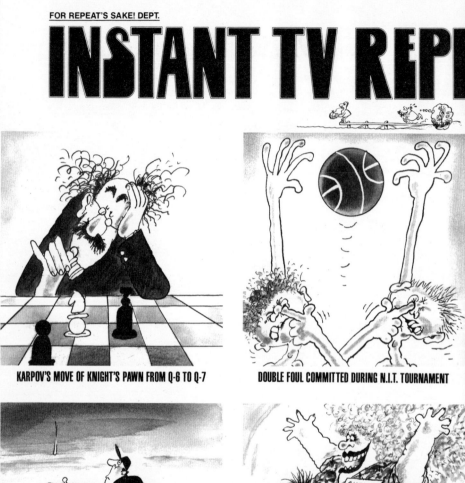

AYS We Would Rather Not Have to See

TIST AND WRITER: PAUL PETER PORGES

FOURTH FALSE START MADE AT THE WANAMAKER MILE

MATING DANCE PERFORMED BY OSTRICHES ON "NOVA"

SPEARING PENALTY INCURRED AT STANLEY CUP PLAYOFF

DESIGNATED HITTER WAITING IN ON-DECK CIRCLE

BOOMERANGLES DEPT.

"Catch 22" was a best-selling book that later was made into a successful movi In case you didn't read the book or see the movie, it was about an Air Forc bombardier who doesn't want to fly any more dangerous missions. Since there' an Air Force regulation which states that if you're insane, you can't fly, ou

MAD'S REAL LI

You've had season tickets to an NFL team for years, and they always lose, but you're afraid of giving up those season tickets because the team might start to win, so you keep on going to the crummy games year after year . . .

. . . but since the stadium is sold out year after year, the owner doesn't have to do anything to improve the team!

You cannot date unless the guy comes to the house so your Father can meet him...

. . . but if he ever meets your date he'll never let you go out with him!

The only way a dentist can find hidde cavities is if he X-rays your teeth . .

The Law says that when you reach the age of 16, you can get your driver's license . . .

. . . but if you drive the family car, his insurance rates will triple, so your Old Man says, "Forget it—until you're 25!"

Your parents, the government and nut tion experts tell you that you're rui ing your health by eating junk food . .

hero tells his shrink that he's crazy and therefore, according to regulations, he doesn't have to fly. But there's a catch — Catch-22 — which states that if you don't want to fly dangerous missions, it proves you're sane — and therefore you have to keep flying! Ridiculous, huh? Well, how about this second collection of

E "CATCH 22'S"

ARTIST: PAUL COKER
WRITER: LOU SILVERSTONE

If you can only get your very own pad, you'll finally be free to do whatever you want without having to ask your parents' permission . . .

. . . but you'll be so busy doing the things your parents did for you, like cooking and cleaning and laundry, etc., that you won't have time to do whatever it was you wanted to do!

. . . but what you can get from X-rays is a helluva lot worse than a cavity!

If you don't give the school bully your lunch money, he'll kill you . . .

. . . but if you do give him your lunch money, you're gonna starve to death!

. . . but if you give up junk food, your health will be totalled by starvation, because that's the only food you like!

If you don't study for exams, you'll flunk and have to spend another year in school—which is unthinkable . . .

. . . but if you do study and graduate, then you'll have to go out and find a job—which is even more unthinkable!

MARKING TIME DEPT.

AND NOW, FOR YOU NOSTALGIA FANS, A LOOK BACK AT

GRAFFITI

ARTIST: BOB CLARKE WRITER: PAUL PETER PORGES

HE OLD DAYS WHEN THINGS WERE A LOT DIFFERENT!

THROUGH HISTORY

FREE
MONTEZUMA

PYTHAGORAS
IS A SQUARE

JUPITER
IS DEAD

Free the
Black Hole of
Calcutta
146

Luther-
Write
on!

ELEPHANT
POWER

JUDAS
KISSES
AND
TELLS

BAN
THE
LEAF

JOKE AND DAGGER DEPT.

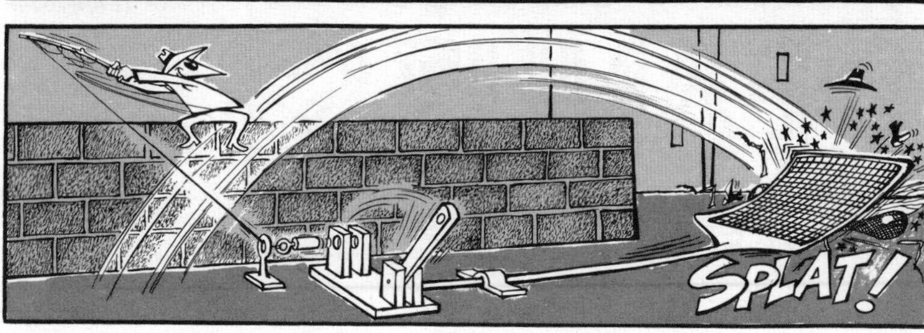

STRIP TEASE DEPT.

In past issues, MAD has presented All-Inclusive, Do-It Yourself versions of Newspaper Stories, Songs, Comedy Routines, etc. Now, for all you "Peanuts" fans who have fun reading the strip, here is your chance to have fun writing it. (Hey, Charlie Schulz! If you want to take a vacation, feel free to take advantage of this clever article!) Simply fill in the numbered balloons from the corresponding numbered lists, and you'll be creating...

MAD'S ALL-INCLUSIVE DO-IT-YOURSELF PEANUTS COMIC STRIP

ARTIST: JACK RICKARD WRITER: FRANK JACOBS

1

YOU'RE A ***BORN LOSER!***

YOUR ***HEAD*** COULD DOUBLE AS A ***SOFTBALL!***

EVERYONE ***ABUSES*** YOU!

YOU GIVE ***LIVING*** A ***BAD NAME!***

YOU'VE GOT A ***PIN-CUSHION*** FOR A ***BRAIN!***

YOU'RE THE ***JOKE*** OF THE ***NEIGHBORHOOD!***

5

IN ***YOUR HONOR!***

TO PAY ***TRIBUTE*** TO YOUR ***LEADERSHIP!***

ON YOUR ***BIRTHDAY!***

SO THE ***GANG*** CAN SHOW YOU HOW WE ***FEEL!***

TO KICK OFF "***CELEBRATE CHARLIE BROWN WEEK***"!

YOU'LL ***REMEMBER*** THE ***REST*** OF YOUR ***LIFE!***

2

TELL ME ALL **ABOUT** IT!

AT **LEAST** I'M FAMOUS FOR **SOMETHING**!

COMING FROM YOU, THAT'S **PRAISE**!

I **LOVE IT** WHEN YOU **SWEET-TALK**!

IT TOOK YOU **25 YEARS** TO FIND **THAT** OUT?

DO YOU KEEP THIS UP FOR **FOUR PANELS**?

3

NOBODY RECOGNIZES YOUR **FINER QUALITIES**!

YOU'RE ADMIRED BY YOUR **FRIENDS** AND **TEAMMATES**!

YOU DESERVE **MUCH BETTER TREATMENT**!

WITHOUT **YOU**, I WOULD BE **NOTHING**!

YOUR **HEART** IS AS **BIG** AS **ALL OUTDOORS**!

YOU'RE **KIND** AND **DECENT** AND **LOYAL**!

4

I MUST BE IN THE **WRONG STRIP**!

WHY ISN'T SHE SUCKING UP TO **SCHROEDER**?

I WISH I WERE **BRIGHT ENOUGH** TO KNOW WHAT SHE'S **UP TO**?

NOBODY'S EVER **THIS** NICE TO ME!

I'VE GOT A **FEELING** THIS IS GOING TO **COST** ME!

I **THINK** I LIKED IT **BETTER** WHEN SHE **DESPISED** ME!

6

A-A **PARTY** FOR **ME**!?

YOU MEAN YOU'RE **NOT SETTING ME UP**?

YOU'VE **SURE CHANGED**!

IT'LL BE **GREAT** GETTING SOME **RESPECT**!

I'LL SURE ENJOY BEING WITH MY **FRIENDS**!

HOW CAN I EVER **THANK** YOU?

7

YOU'RE NOT INVITED!

IT'S ON THE DAY YOU'RE **OUT OF TOWN**!

THE PARTY WAS **YESTERDAY**!

YOU'LL BE THE **ONLY** ONE **THERE**!

I WAS **TESTING** TO SEE HOW **GULLIBLE** YOU ARE!

I'M **TELLING** EVERYONE IT'S FOR **LINUS**!

8

I'LL **KILL** MYSELF!

MAYBE I SHOULD **RETIRE**!

I'LL GO HOME AND **BEAT UP SNOOPY**!

I NEED **DEEP THERAPY**!

I'LL PUT A **CONTRACT** OUT ON HER!

I'LL TRY REPLACING **ANDY CAPP**!

ERR APPARENT DEPT.

Recently, we asked one of our idiot artists to do a draw
of a School Prom. Unfortunately, he didn't do a very go

HOW MANY MISTAKES CA

job. In fact, he made a lot of mistakes...20 in all. And now, it's up to you to find them. So c'mon! Let's see...

YOU FIND IN THIS PICTURE?

ANSWERS

1. The teachers are not making asses of themselves on the dance floor.
2. Collectively, there is less than $20,000 worth of orthodontia in this room.
3. The Varsity Football jock is carrying on an intelligent conversation.
4. This guy married his high-school sweetheart *before* she got pregnant.
5. The guy bragging about the number of girls he's gone to bed with is telling the truth.
6. The teenager is having a tough time finding a drug connection.
7. The two girls who discovered that they're wearing the same dress are still having a good time.
8. The Drama Major is not talking only about herself.
9. The guy's mustache took him less then nine months to grow.
10. This guy respects this girl for her mind.
11. The guy patting his friend on the back did not stick a "Kick Me!" sign there.
12. The guy who invited the girl home to hear his stereo really wants her to hear his stereo.
13. Students are refusing to buy the answers to the upcoming finals.
14. This guy realizes that he's too drunk to drive.
15. The Photographer is not taking a picture while the couple blinks.
16. The student wearing sneakers with his tuxedo feels out of place.
17. The girl wearing the "D" cup bra actually *needs* a "D" cup bra.
18. The students have tied their ties without help from their fathers.
19. The teenager pretending to be drunk is actually drunk.
20. There are no food-fights going on at the buffet table.

ARTIST: ANGELO TORRES

WRITER: CHRIS HART

AUDUBON-BONS DEPT.

A MAD LOOK

AT BIRDS

ARTIST & WRITER: SERGIO ARAGONES

PETRIFIED
FOREST

SPLAT!
AMAN
VREDE
ARAGONÉS

VANISHING AMERICANISMS DEPT.

HAS ANYBODY EV

A DUNCE CAP

OR A BURGLAR WEARING A "LONE RANGER" MASK

OR A NEWSBOY YELLING "EXTRA! READ ALL ABOUT IT!"

OR A MAGICI

TIED TO THE END OF A STICK

OR AN INDIAN THAT EVER SAID "HOW!"

OR A LADY FLIRTING WITH A MAN BY DROPPING HER HANDKERCHIEF

IN A DOOR

OR TWO DRUNKS STAGGERING UP THE STREET SINGING "

OR A BILLY GOAT EATING A TIN CAN

OR THE "LIFE OF THE PARTY" W

ED OUT WITH SOAP

OR A MAN DRINK CHAMPAGNE FROM A LADY'S SH

WAITING FOR HER HUSBAND WITH A ROLLING PIN

OR A REPORTER WIT

R REALLY SEEN...

ARTIST: GEORGE WOODBRIDGE WRITER: LARRY SHARP

OR SOMEONE THROWING AN OLD SHOE AT A CAT ON A FENCE

EVER SAID "ABRA CADABRA" OR A HOBO WITH HIS BELONGINGS

!" OR A JUG OF WHISKEY WITH "XXX" MARKED ON IT

FE FALLING FROM A HIGH WINDOW OR A SALESMAN PUT HIS FOOT

DELINE" OR A ST. BERNARD WITH A KEG OF BRANDY

A LAMPSHADE ON HIS HEAD OR A KID GETTING HIS MOUTH WASH-

OR "STARS" WHEN YOU'RE HIT ON THE HEAD OR A WIFE

ESS" CARD STUCK IN HIS HAT BAND OR A FUNNY ARTICLE IN MAD?

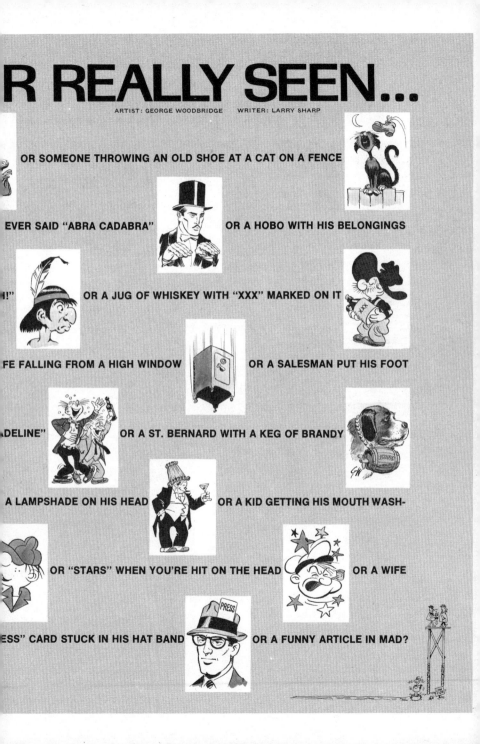

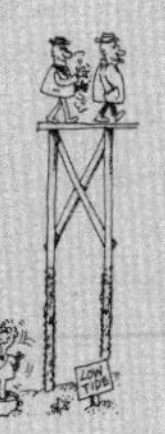

HOP, SKIP AND SQUISH DEPT.

We've read that people who live in big cities are becoming soft and flabby because of limite opportunities for sports and exercise. Well, we at MAD say that's ridiculous. People wh

UNAVOIDABLE EXERCISES

ARTIST: AL JAFFEE

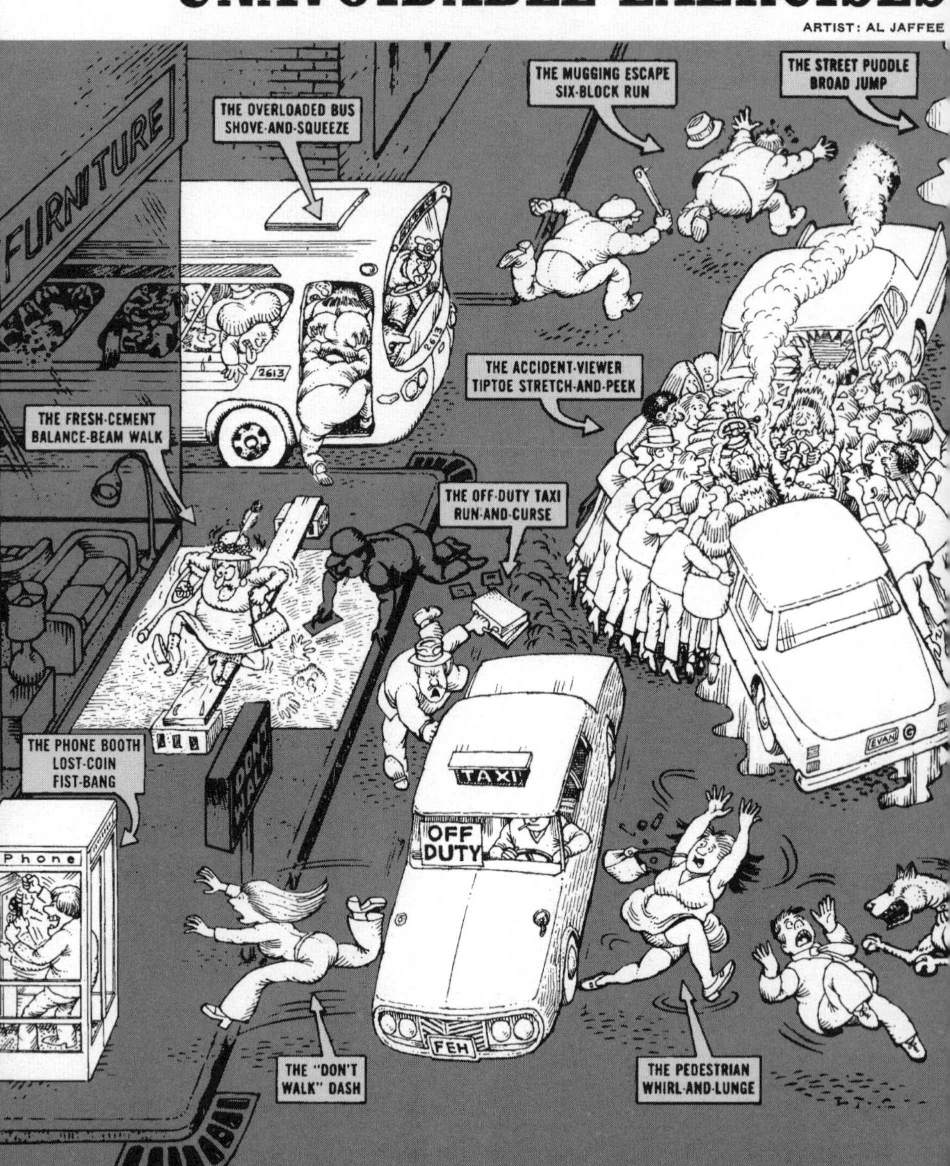

e in cities get all sorts of exercise without even realizing it. As a matter of fact, they n't avoid getting exercise, as you'll see in this panorama, depicting many and varied . . .

OR THE URBAN DWELLER

RITER: FRANK JACOBS

THE PURSE-SNATCH TUG OF WAR

THE DESERTED ALLEY RAPID RIGHT-AND-LEFT NECK TURN

THE EIGHT-STORY POWER-FAILURE CLIMB

THE MODERN TAXI SQUEEZE-AND-ENTER

THE SIDEWALK ELEVATOR BACK FLIP

THE INNOCENT BYSTANDER DIVE-AND-COWER

THE DOBERMAN FULL-BODY TURN AND CRINGE

THE DOGGIE-DO HOP-SKIP-AND-JUMP

MAY THE FOES BE WITH YOU DEPT.

One of the keys to the success of the Rocky series is the thrilling, charismatic villains Sly Stallone invents: Apollo Creed! Clubber Lang! Drago! But who's left? Where are Rocky's next opponents going to come from? We think Sly plans to pilfer old movies for Bad Guys to fight. Here are the scenerios for...

ROCKY V, VI, VII, VIII, IX, X, XI OR, THE ITALIAN SCALLION VS THE GREAT HOLLYWOOD VILLAINS

ARTIST AND WRITER: TOM HACHTMAN

THE ROCKY OF OZ

In his first musical, Rocky, the lovable boxer without a brain, battles Margaret Hamilton, The Wicked Witch of The West! In the closing seconds of the fight, Rocky is saved from being counted out when a giant tornado picks up the Champ, carries him over the rainbow, and dumps him back in South Philly!

ROCKY BATTLES THE EMPIRE

It's Rocky vs the heavy breather of the universe, Darth Vader! On the night of the fight, Rock learns that Darth (aka "Lazer Fists") is really Don King! Can Rocky call on "The Force" in time to save the Boxing Federation? Is Don King Rock's long lost father? May the fists be with you in this battle of slow wit vs evil!

ROCKYDEUS

In this lavish costume drama, Rocky mocks his rival Salieri by donning boxing gloves and pounding out one of the poor man's bland melodies on the clavier. Salieri beseeches God, "Why did you choose this moronic brute for such gifts and not me?!" This is the cultural Rocky film the critics have been asking for!

ROCKY THE THIRTEENTH

ɪcky suffers his most brutal beating when he meets the summer mp champ, Jason, "The Mutilator"! Will this battle of the quels really be "The Final Chapter"?? A blood lover's delight!

JOHN CARPENTER'S THE THING IN THE RING

All of Rocky's former foes merge into one big, mutating lump and return for a rematch. If Rock isn't careful this slithering "Thing" will mimic his cellular structure and Rocky movies will never be the same—or just possibly more alike than ever!

ROCKY FLEW OVER THE CUCKOO'S NEST

ɔcky fakes being punch-drunk to get into psychiatric hospital r a rest. But once in, he faces his meanest opponent yet—urse Cratchett! In round one, Big Nurse gives Rock a dose of edication! In round four, she zaps him with electro-shock! round 10, she hits him with a frontal lobotomy! Will any this punishment have a noticeable effect on the Champ??

ROCKY DEAREST

Faye Dunaway is charming as Joan Crawford—until the blood starts to spill! The minute one itsy bitsy drop soils the spotless canvas, Rocky finds himself down for the count—scrubbing the mat! As the referee cries, "NO WIRE HANGERS!" a dazed Rocky wonders if this could be his last tangle!

BIG-NAME BRANDS DEPT.

Who would have ever thought that one day you'd be able to walk into a grocery store and find Paul Newman's face on a bottle of salad dressing or spaghetti sauce? We wonder, can it be long before other famou personalities follow Paul's lead and intr duce products of their own? In the futur iccess in show business no longer

MAD'S CELEBRIT

BRONSON
T.V. DINNER
The frozen meals for those with a Death Wish

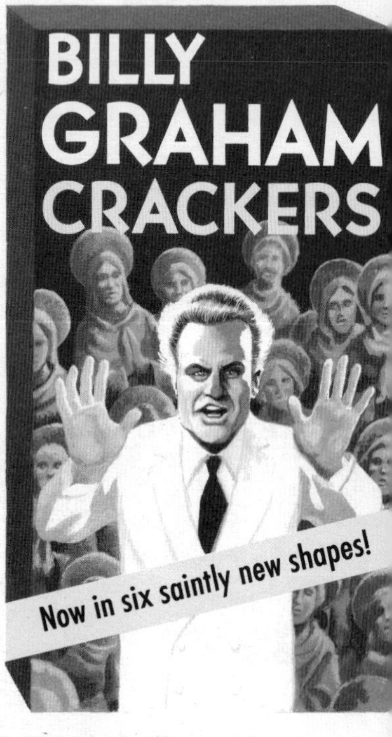

BILLY
GRAHAM
CRACKERS
Now in six saintly new shapes!

John
CANDY
BAR
MAKES A Splash IN YOUR STOMACH!
1,000 CALORIES IN EVERY BITE!

WOW!

Burt Reynolds Wrap
the only aluminum foil that's wrapped up in itself!

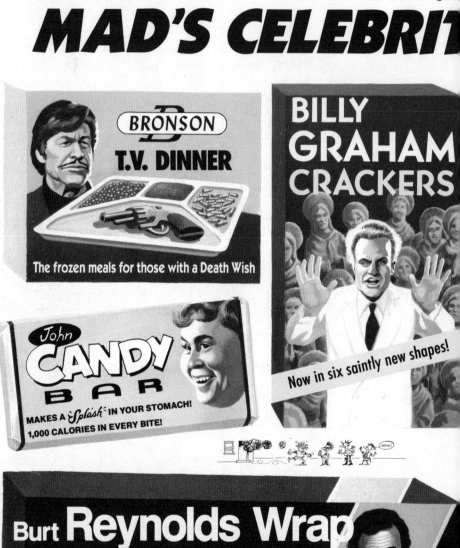

measured by the number of hit movies, TV shows or records someone has, but rather by the number of products featuring their face and name on the labels? If your answer to our last question is yes (or even maybe) then grab your cents-off coupons and look for a shopping cart with four wheels that work! You're ready to join us on a tour of

Y SUPERMARKET

ARTIST: BOB CLARKE WRITERS: JOE RAIOLA & CHARLIE KADAU

MARK
Virginia
HAMILL
MAY THE PORK BE WITH YOU!

ALPHABETTE
MIDLER
SOUP MIX
50 OFF-COLOR WORDS
IN EVERY BOWL!
CENSORED!
CENSORED!
CENSORED!
CENSORED!
CENSORED!
CENSORED!
CENSORED!
CENSORED!

ARNOLD
SCHWARZEN
EGG
ROLLS
STRONG FLAVOR
FAT FREE
ADDS MUSCLE TO EVERY MEAL! STRONG FLAVOR! FAT FREE!

BRYANT
GUMBALLS
TRY ONE TODAY-SHOW YOUR FRIENDS

NEW! EASY TO PREPARE! TAKES JUST 48 HRS!
SPAGHETTI
MURPHY

Steven SPIEL
BURGERS

Every mouthful produces a special effect!

AL
CAPPACINO
Make them a coffee they can't refuse!
TASTY UNDERWORLD FLAVOR

Stevie
WONDER
BREAD
For once in my life I have someone who kneads me!

DON MARTIN DEPT.

On A Saturday Afternoon

THE EERIE OF RELATIVITY DEPT.

In issue No. 180 (Jan. '76), we ran an article we didn't think very much of! But we were wrong. People wrote in and told us how much they loved it. And so, sinc

TIME FLIES...TI

TIME FLIES...

...when you're playing a video game.

TIME DRAGS...

...when your friend is playing it.

TIME FLIES...

...during your summer vacation.

ARTIST: PAUL COKEF

TIME FLIES...

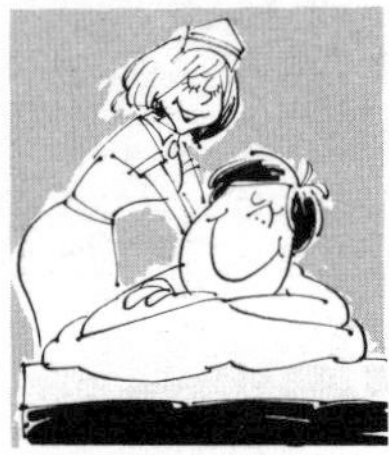

...when a beautiful nurse is giving you a rub-down.

TIME DRAGS...

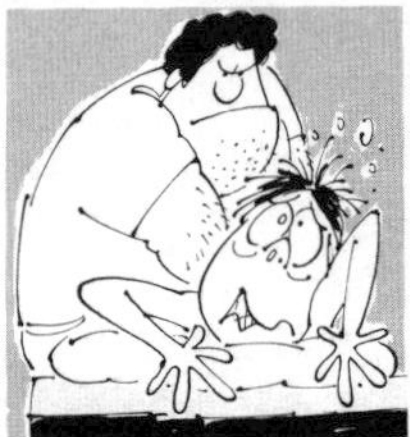

...when a male nurse is giving you a rub-down..

TIME DRAGS...

...when you're waiting for the phone to ring.

TIME FLIES...

...when you're trying to answer it before the caller hangs up.

TIME FLIES...

...between the times you have to take your dog out.

TIME DRAGS...

...while you're waiting for him to finish what you took him out to do.

TIME FLIES...

...when you're in a deep sleep.

we're very sensitive to our readers' likes and dislikes, we're running this new version of the article, a mere seven years later! And you thought we didn't care!

IE DRAGS... (AND VICE VERSA)

TIME DRAGS...

...until the next one starts.

TIME FLIES...

...when you take a final exam.

TIME DRAGS...

...when you wait for the results.

WRITER: STAN HART

TIME DRAGS...

...when you're waiting for the girl to get undressed.

TIME FLIES...

...when she is undressed.

TIME DRAGS...

...between bank deposits.

TIME FLIES...

...between bank withdrawals.

TIME DRAGS...

...when you have insomnia.

TIME DRAGS...

...when you wait for the pizza to go from "boiling" to just "red hot."

TIME FLIES...

...when the same pizza goes from "red hot" to "ice cold."

YOU KNOW YOU'RE IN A SECOND MARRIAGE WHEN...

. . . she insists that her diamond engagement ring be a lot larger than the one you gave your first wife.

YOU KNOW YOU'RE IN A SECOND MARRIAGE WHEN...

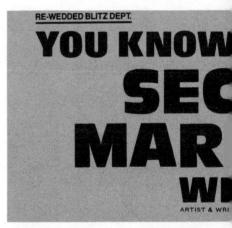

. . . he comes home with a bouquet of "Happy Anniversary" flowers . . . and it's the date of his *former* anniversary.

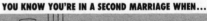

YOU KNOW YOU'RE IN A SECOND MARRIAGE WHEN...

. . . you have to go to work in order to make ends meet because of your Husband's incredible alimony payments.

YOU KNOW YOU'RE IN A SECOND MARRIAGE WHEN...

. . . you suddenly see trouble and heartache ahead as your kids and his kids start a huge fight . . . at your wedding.

RE-WEDDED BLITZ DEPT.

YOU KNOW SEC MAR WI

ARTIST & WRI

YOU KNOW YOU'RE IN A SECOND MARRIAGE WHEN...

. . . you find yourself stuck with amusing his kids when they visit him on Sunday . . . while he watches football.

YOU KNOW YOU'RE IN A SECOND MARRIAGE WHEN...

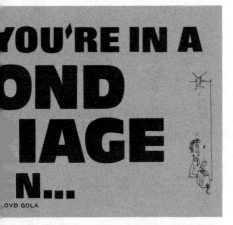

. . . your Wife told you everything before you were married . . . except that her Son is the drummer in a Punk Rock Band.

YOU KNOW YOU'RE IN A SECOND MARRIAGE WHEN...

. . . your Husband told you everything before you were married . . . except that his Daughter runs with the "Hell's Angels".

YOU'RE IN A OND IAGE N...

OYD GOLA

YOU KNOW YOU'RE IN A SECOND MARRIAGE WHEN...

. . . your new Mother-In-Law keeps calling you "Nancy". . . and your name is Mary Lou!

YOU KNOW YOU'RE IN A SECOND MARRIAGE WHEN...

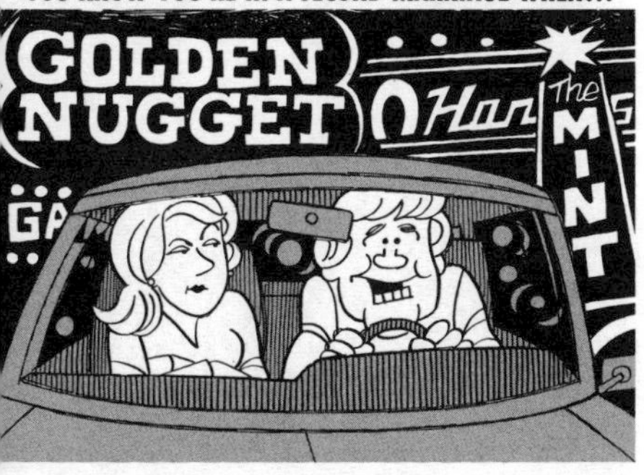

. . . he raves about the fun you had the last time you were in Las Vegas . . . and you've never been to Las Vegas before.

YOU KNOW YOU'RE IN A SECOND MARRIAGE WHEN...

. . . you are horrified to discover that your second Husband is actually starting to make your first Husband look good.

THERE'S BULL IN THEM BULLETINS DEPT.

Here we go with another vital MAD Public Service Feature ...this one designed to instruct you in the tricky art of

INTERPRETING THE NEWS

WRITER: GARY ALEXANDER

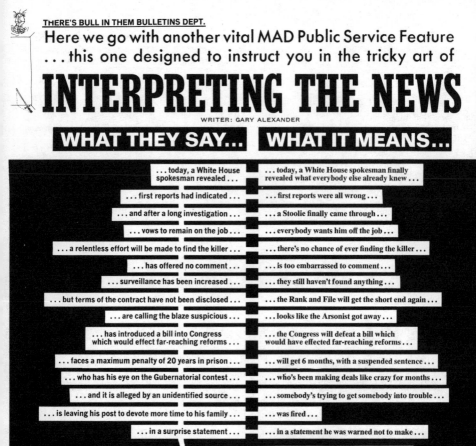

WHAT THEY SAY...	WHAT IT MEANS...
...today, a White House spokesman revealed...	...today, a White House spokesman finally revealed what everybody else already knew...
...first reports had indicated...	...first reports were all wrong...
...and after a long investigation...	...a Stoolie finally came through...
...vows to remain on the job...	...everybody wants him off the job...
...a relentless effort will be made to find the killer...	...there's no chance of ever finding the killer...
...has offered no comment...	...is too embarrassed to comment...
...surveillance has been increased...	...they still haven't found anything...
...but terms of the contract have not been disclosed...	...the Rank and File will get the short end again...
...are calling the blaze suspicious...	...looks like the Arsonist got away...
...has introduced a bill into Congress which would effect far-reaching reforms...	...the Congress will defeat a bill which would have effected far-reaching reforms...
...faces a maximum penalty of 20 years in prison...	...will get 6 months, with a suspended sentence...
...who has his eye on the Gubernatorial contest...	...who's been making deals like crazy for months...
...and it is alleged by an unidentified source...	...somebody's trying to get somebody into trouble...
...is leaving his post to devote more time to his family...	...was fired...
...in a surprise statement...	...in a statement he was warned not to make...

PHOTO BY: UPI

FROM TOPPS TO BOTTOM DEPT.

In major league baseball it doesn't matter how lousy a player you are—even the most anemic scrub is qualified to be immortalized in a baseball card, while some of the game's most integral characters will never know 3X5 cardboard fame! It's time this gross injustice was corrected by adopting MAD's suggestions for...

LUCKY THE LEECH

TEAM MASCOT

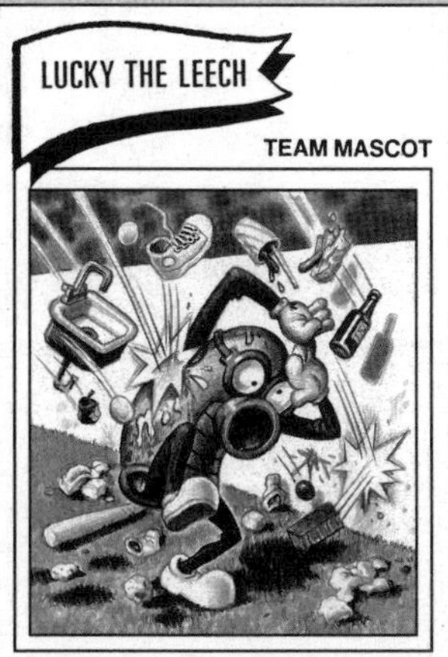

LUCKY THE LEECH

TEAM MASCOT

Fun Facts: The amount of garbage and junk food thrown at Lucky by the fans during a typical homestand would feed the Republic of Tunisia for one year.

Everyone who has ever donned the Lucky mascot suit has died of heat prostration within 36 hours of taking the job.

Quote: *"Okay, fans! Give me a 'J'! Hey, c'mon, give me a 'J'! Let's go—ow! Stop kicking me! Help!"*

MAKING BASEBALL CARD COLLECTIONS COMPLETE

A Tribute To Our National Pastime's Unsung Heroes

ARTIST: JOHN POUND

WRITER: DESMOND DEVLIN

PHIL RONZONI

TEAM ANNOUNCER

PHIL RONZONI

TEAM ANNOUNCER

Fun Facts: Was behind the mike for a record 17 consecutive games without once announcing the score.

His campy singing of "Take Me Out to the Ballgame" during the seventh inning stretch never fails to inspire any true fan to cast a teary eye toward the broadcast booth and say, "Now I know what death is like."

Quote: *"Mmmm-mm, these crumb buns from Sal's bakery are great. I believe they've been heated up... Hey, what's that man doing on third? Did a run score? Bernie, what happened?"*

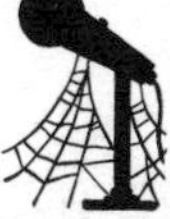

KURT KOLLINS

PLAYER AGENT

KURT "KOUGH IT UP" KOLLINS

PLAYER AGENT

Fun Facts: Had an incentive clause inserted in Dave Whiffle's contract which gave him an extra $200,000 for "coming to play."

When "Kough It Up" heard an announcer claim that his client, Wally Joyride, always gave 110%, he demanded a 10% hike in Joyride's salary (and in his commission)!

Quote: *"I deserve my money. I hammer out agreements, meet with owners, check the stock market and chase down sponsors. All my clients do is play baseball!"*

MARGO ADDLED

ROAD TRIP BIMBO

CHAUNCEY GALOOT

IDIOT FAN

CHAUNCEY GALOOT

IDIOT FAN

Fun Facts: Painted a baseball onto his face which wouldn't come off for two months; the incident cost him his job as circuit court judge.

Shows his enthusiasm when home team scores a run by firing a small cannon filled with beer, sauerkraut and pizza crusts on unsuspecting fans sitting below.

Quote: *"No, I need something that says, 'class.' How about the Elephant Man rubber mask?"*

"SQUINTY" LONGSTREET

UMPIRE

VINCE ALONZO

BOOKIE

VINCE "SNAKE EYES" ALONZO

BOOKIE

Fun Facts: Lost two million bucks to former manager Pete Moss; won back twice that much by laying 3-to-1 at his legal hearing.

Cleared a fortune at his local movie theater in 1988 by getting suckers to bet on the Black Sox in *Eight Men Out*.

Quote: *"My proudest contribution to baseball is inventing the Tommy Lasorda Body Wizard Over-Under Bet!"*

WALLY ALZHEIMER

USHER

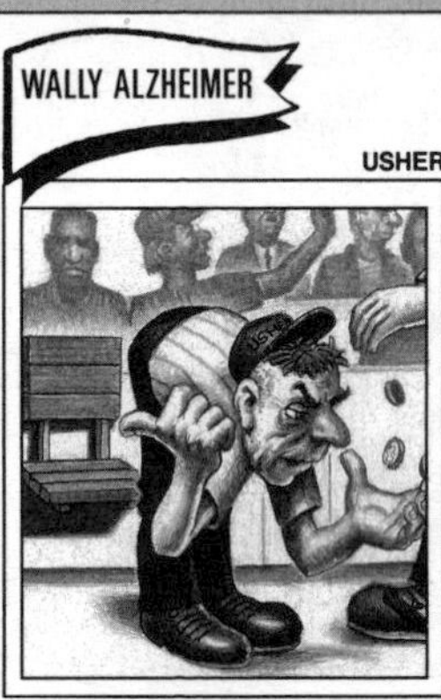

MARGO ADDLED

ROAD TRIP BIMBO

Fun Facts: As part of her 50–50 settlement, demanded that she be credited in the official league stat book with 108 of Suede Bugs' 216 hits in 1989.

Margo was "appalled" at the sensational media circus that publicized only the cheap, smutty aspects of her story, and said so in an interview in *Panthouse Magazine,* where she appeared naked.

Quote: *"I'll be able to correct that hitch in your stroke as soon as we check the films."*

RICHARD MILHOUS SPINEGRABBER

TEAM OWNER

RICHARD MILHOUS SPINEGRABBER XIII

TEAM OWNER, NEW YORK—NEW JERSEY—DENVER—PHOENIX—OKEEFENOKEE YANKOVICHS

Fun Facts: Last September, he canceled Fan Appreciation Day, kept all the ticket money, and told the fans he really appreciated it.

He's moved his team so often that there are skidmarks on home plate; pioneered the first Port-A-Stadium.

Quote: *Complimented on his big fat money belt, he said, "But I'm not wearing any belt!"*

"SQUINTY" LONGSTREET

UMPIRE

Fun Facts: The somewhat plump "Squinty" was able to assist the Pittsburgh field crew last season during a rain delay by covering the pitcher's mound with a pair of his shorts.

He got such a thrill from bumping manager Pete Moss during a heated argument that the two bought a bungalow when the season ended.

Quote: *"Is it four strikes and three balls, or the other way around?"*

ANDY ANABOLIC

TEAM DOCTOR

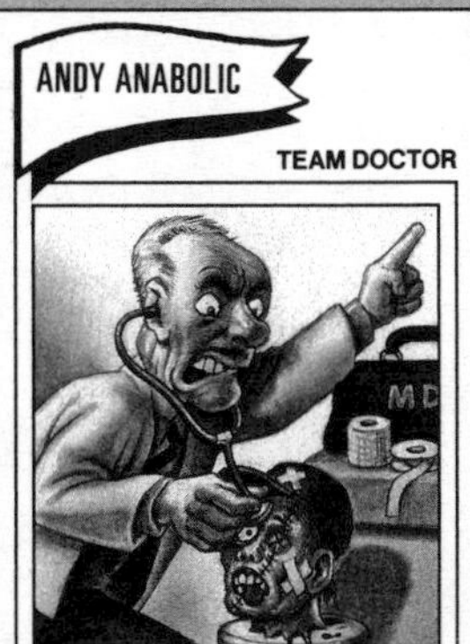

ANDY ANABOLIC

TEAM DOCTOR

Fun Facts: Once called off an operation on account of rain and covered his patient with a tarp.

First doctor to offer free checkups for fans on "Groin Pull Night."

Quote: *"Get out there and play, you've got another lung!"*

WALLY ALZHEIMER

USHER

Fun Facts: Because he feels that baseball's past is its finest legacy, Wally hasn't cleaned his seat rag since 1978.

Alzheimer boasts the only toupee in the game that is actually made out of artificial turf.

Quote: *"Hey you! Yes, you with the semi-automatic rifle! Lemme check your stub!"*

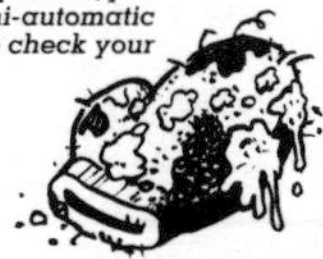

POINDEXTER SABERMETRIC

STATISTICIAN

POINDEXTER SABERMETRIC

STATISTICIAN

Fun Facts: Can compute any player's stolen bases/caught stealing ratio in seconds, yet doesn't know who won the World Series last year.

Poindexter sells stats to agents for contract negotiations that conclusively prove why most players are "uncrowned MVPs," and sells stats to the owners that prove those same players are uncoordinated schmucks!

Quote: *"Every time I watch* Pride of the Yankees *I cry, not so much because Lou Gehrig dies but because I might've paid sixty bucks for him in rotisserie!"*

HAND SHAKEDOWN DEPT.

A MAD LOOK AT PAL

M READING

ARTIST & WRITER: SERGIO ARAGONES

BE KIND TO ANNUALS DEPT.

THINGS YOU
YOUR DOG ON

Let him throw his very own party!

Give him a full day of belly-scratching!

Perform a trick for him!

Play "Happy Birthday" on a high-pitched dog whistle!

Give him the use of your lounger for the day!

Help him dig holes in your neighbor's lawn!

:AN DO FOR IIS BIRTHDAY

WRITER AND ARTIST: PAUL PETER PORGES

Share his hobby with him!

Dress up as a mailman and let him chase you!

Walk him the very moment he wants you to!

Let him sleep where he wants to!

Have a drink with him at his private bar!

Collect several weeks of garbage for him to go through!

LORD OF THE BUNGLE DEPT.

A MAD LOOK

ARTIST: JACK DA

AT TARZAN

WRITER: DON EDWING

NYAHH
NEE YAH
OOOOHAH
THUMP
THUMP

HELP!

HELP!

NYAH
OOOHA

OOOK!
OOOK!

SPLAT
Man . . . you're lucky you didn't cut your **head** off!

AAEEOoo

For Outstanding Achievement In Stretching A "Two-Hour Idea" Into A Five-Part Mini-Series

Best Performance By An Actor Or Actress In A Talk Show "Plug" For A Failing Series

STATUES OF LIMITATIONS DEPT.

TV EMMY AWARDS

Best Dramatic Series Kept On By A Network As An Example of "Quality Programming"...Despite The Fact That No One Ever Watches It

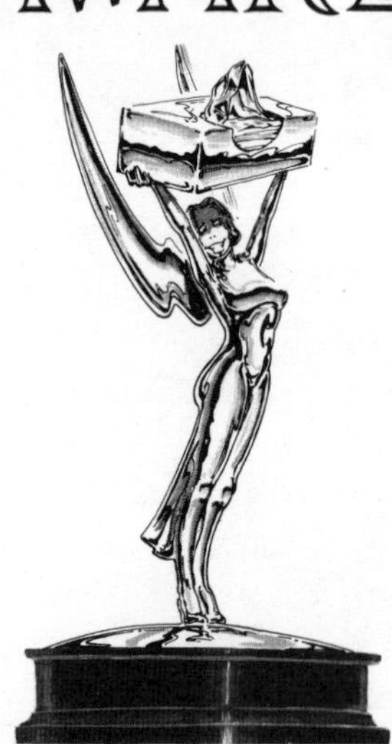

For Outstanding Achievement In Creating A Maudlin, Tear-Jerking Scene In A SitCom When The Writers Couldn't Think Of A Funny Ending

Outstanding Achievement In SitCom Writing For the Best-Disguised "Re-Working" Of An Old "I Love Lucy" Plot

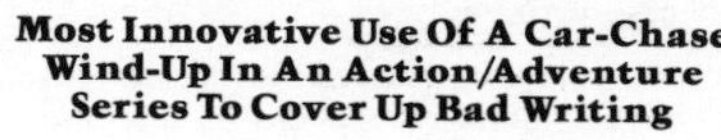

Most Innovative Use Of A Car-Chase Wind-Up In An Action/Adventure Series To Cover Up Bad Writing

WE'D LIKE TO SEE

ARTIST: MICHAEL MONTGOMERY WRITER: MIKE SNIDER

Best Scene Or Line Of Dialogue Used Out-Of-Context In A Network Promo To Make A Show Look More Titillating Than It Actually Is

For Outstanding Achievement In Packing A Dramatic Show Episode With Over-The-Hill "Guest Stars" That Nobody's Heard Of For Over Ten Years

DRIVE SHAFTS DEPT.

Are you getting bored with those tiresome bumper sticker messages you see on just about every car these days? It's time to strike back! How?? For each idiotic message you cannot stand, write an

SNAPPY ANSWERS TO S

*ANY SIMILARITY TO AL JAFFEE'S POPULAR "SNAPPY ANSWER

RECYCLERS DO IT MORE THAN ONCE

SO DO *LITTERERS*, ONLY THEY DO IT *SLOPPIER!*

AMERICA... *LOVE IT OR LEAVE IT*

I ONLY SORT OF *LIKE* IT!
CAN I LIVE ON THE CANADIAN BORDER?

MY OTHER CAR IS A **PORSCHE**

NOT ANY MORE! I JUST **STOLE** IT!

I brake for **ANIMALS**

WONDERFUL! Now, how about braking for people?

I ♥ MY DOG

THAT'S NOT A NICE THING TO CALL YOUR GIRL!

appropriate "comeback" on a sticker of your own. Then, when you spot an offending car, ride along-side of it with your corresponding zinger! We'll show you what we mean with these MAD examples of

UPID BUMPER STICKERS*

JPID QUESTIONS" IS PURELY BECAUSE WE SWIPED IT!

ARTIST: BOB CLARKE WRITER: LARRY SIEGEL

HAVE YOU HUGGED YOUR WIFE LATELY?
NO! I'M HAVING TOO MUCH FUN WITH YOURS!
I'd rather be SKIING
THE WAY YOU DRIVE, I THOUGHT YOU WERE!
IF YOU CAN READ THIS, YOU'RE DRIVING TOO CLOSE
IF YOUR STICKER WAS BIGGER, I WOULDN HAVE TO DRIVE SO CLOSE TO READ IT!
I ♥ N.Y.
SO DID I TILL A MUGGER ♣ED ME AND GRABBED MY ♦S
ONE NUCLEAR BOMB CAN RUIN YOUR WHOLE DAY
ONE BOMB BUMPER STICKER JUST RUINED MINE!

CRASH COURSE DEPT.

Some of you hot shots have probably taken a "Drivers Ed" course, and maybe even passed a written exam to get your state license. So now you think you're ready to climb behind the wheel and handle any situation that comes up, eh? Well, we've got news for you, Booby! All those rules you learned, about slowing down at deer crossings and avoiding

THE MAD PRACTI

1. If you suddenly realize that you are driving the wrong way on a one-way street, you should…

A. start driving backwards a whole lot faster than the oncoming traffic is moving forward.______
B. prepare to tell the policeman that you're from England, where driving rules are all the opposite of ours.______
C. switch into the lane reserved for oncoming buses, and start to pray that you're on a route that has lousy, infrequent service.______

2. When you pass the scene of an accident and see law officers waiving the traffic through…

A. stop and thank the policemen for kindly pointing out the grisly sight to you.______
B. pass on by as directed, but then "rubberneck" by staring into your rear-view mirror for the next half a mile.______
C. plow into the accident so you can collect from the insurance companies of the other drivers involved.______

3. When driving with a back seat full of restless children…

A. turn around and look each one in the eye while scolding them, so they will know you mean business.______
B. take your hands off the wheel long enough to grab the worst offender by the throat, and shake him until his teeth rattle.______
C. twist the steering wheel sharply back and forth, so the kids will be too busy picking themselves up off the floor to whine.______

7. Upon realizing that you've just slammed and locked your car door with the only car keys inside…

A. pay the thief who's breaking into a nearby car to break into yours.______
B. climb in through the sun roof. If your car doesn't have a sun roof, go buy a can opener at a nearby store so you can install one.______
C. do what everyone else does: stand there staring through the side window at your keys as if that's going to help somehow.______

8. If you accidentally drop a lighted cigarette while the car is in motion;

A. roll down your windows and immediately drive through a car wash.______
B. roll up your windows and proceed, knowing that the fire will go out as soon as it has used up all the oxygen inside the vehicle.______
C. immediately slip off your shoes, because it's a lot easier to locate something hot on the car floor when you're barefoot.______

9. If your contact lens should pop out while you're driving at high speed, you should immediately…

A. shut your eyes, because seeing only fuzzy images of oncoming traffic is dangerous.______
B. speed up, so you can reach your destination quickly and begin looking for your lost lens.______
C. dive to the floor and hunt for it, since you can no longer see anything through the windshield anyway.______

eft turns into fire stations, will only be of use to you once or twice in your driving lifetime. You haven't really been tested or even informed about the practical driving decisions you'll be required to make every day. Lucky for you MAD has corrected this terrible oversight. Quiz yourself and discover the motoring skills you lack with

CAL DRIVING TEST

ARTIST: PAUL COKER WRITER: TOM KOCH

4. To avoid being delayed by meandering senior citizens in crosswalks...

A. blow your horn suddenly, and then drive under them when they all jump straight up into the air.________

B. open the passenger door and graciously offer to drive them to the nearest curb.________

C. Always carry a bullhorn so you'll be prepared to announce that Hugh Downs is autographing free copies of the Readers Digest for all who hurry over to the Community Center.________

5. If your car conks out in a strange town, and you're broke...

A. find a temporary job in the area to earn money for the repair bill. Anything that pays over $1000 a week should be adequate.________

B. try to map out a route home that's downhill all the way, so you won't need an engine that runs.________

C. push your car into the nearest vacant lot and prepare to live there until you hear that you've come into a large inheritance.________

6. When flagged down by a policeman for failing to come to a complete stop at a "full stop" sign...

A. tell him you have such a souped-up engine that your car goes 20 miles an hour in neutral.________

B. say something in any foreign language, so he'll assume you didn't know what the word on the sign meant.________

C. confuse him by citing Einstein's Theory to prove that nothing in the universe ever comes to a complete stop.________

10. If you see red lights flashing to warn you that a bridge is out...

A. suggest to the flagman that he tighten his light bulbs so they'll stop blinking.________

B. remember what Burt Reynolds always does and speed up, so you can hurtle across the river without needing a bridge.________

C. roll up the windows before proceeding, so your car will float longer after it hits the water.________

11. The best way to take revenge on a rude motorist is to...

A. point frantically at his rear tire until worry forces him to stop and check out the situation.________

B. take down his license number and then report his car to the police as a stolen vehicle.________

C. flash a phony badge, gesture to him to pull over, and then whiz on past him when he complies.________

12. If you decide to park in a space that's marked with this symbol...

A. prepare to tell the judge that you thought the sign meant "Absolutely No Unicycle Parking".________

B. tell anybody who glares at you that your disability doesn't show because it's mental (and dangerous).________

C. immediately put the hood up, so you can claim that your car is disabled, even if you're not.________

13. If you become involved in a "fender bender" accident that is clearly your fault...

A. announce that you have plenty of collision insurance, and then give the other driver the name of a fictitious insurance company.______
B. make light of the damage you've caused by insisting that his crushed grill can easily be snapped back into place.______
C. suggest that your victim take off before your armed bodyguard arrives to "handle things" for you.______

14. When required to drive the family cat to the veterinarian all alone...

A. wear a bird cage over your head for protection, in case Kitty panics and starts clawing everything in sight.______
B. be alert for special problems if you step on the brake pedal suddenly and feel your foot come down on something warm and soft and furry.______
C. stuff the cat into the glove compartment, and then drive at top speed to reach your destination before the air supply gives out.______

15. When you're late for work and try to finish dressing while driving...

A. at least put on your trousers before leaving the house, because that's impossible to do while operating a moving motor vehicle.______
B. be sure to stay off cobblestone streets while applying lipstick, unless you're satisfied to look like an Amazonian witch doctor.______
C. never apply false eyelashes on the freeway, because a thumb seen at that close range can easily be mistaken for a flesh-colored tanker truck.______

16. When leaving your car parked in a sunny spot makes your steering wheel to hot to touch, you should...

A. Press the mysterious button marked "Cruise Control" and hope that it's some kind of device that enables the car to steer itself.______
B. Obtain enough dimes from a nearby bank to feed the parking meter until evening, when the sun will probably go down.______
C. tell your pesky little brother who always wants to drive your car that you've finally decided to let him.______

17. When the driver behind you honks because you failed to notice that the red light just turned to green...

A. glance in the mirror to check the size and gender of the honker before deciding whether or not to make an issue of this.______
B. give the familiar obscene gesture to indicate that you still consider yourself to be superior to him, even though you tend to daydream.______
C. jump out and hand the other driver a dollar, explaining that it's your payment for wasting five seconds of his valuable time.______

18. In case of disabling car trouble on along a busy interstate highway...

A. stay in your parked car with the windows rolled up and the doors locked, because it's better to die of suffocation than be knifed by a passing maniac.______
B. choose the most annoying passenger in your group to walk to a gas station for help.______
C. leave your car in the highway lane where you stalled, so that the first car that comes along will push you into the next town at 60mph.______

INSTRUCTIONS FOR GRADING YOURSELF

The correct answer to each odd-numbered question is "C". The correct answer to each even-numbered question is "A". Except for questions numbered 4, 10, 12, and 16, where this is not the case, as any fool can see. Credit yourself with 8 percentage points for each correct answer. We realize, of course, that this would give you a total score of 144 percent if you got them all right. However, you couldn't have done that, because all of the multiple choices for at least seven of the questions have been scientifically programmed to be wrong anyway. So there!

DON MARTIN DEPT.

WHILE CLAMMING IN NEW JERSEY

CHOW MEIN LINERS DEPT.

The idea of Fortune Cookies dates back thousands of years. Unfortunately, so do most of the fortunes you find in them. They're usually filled with boring words of wisdom like "The seed of Knowledge that falls upon a barren mind will not flower!" or "The wise man will learn from his mistakes!" Well, it seems to us that people living in the "Now Generation" need

SAVE OUR FORESTS! PLEASE RETURN THIS FORTUNE TO YOUR WAITER FOR RE-CYCLING!

V.D. IS ONE SECRET YOU SHOULD NOT SPREAD AROUND.

As you sit here eating, there is a 75% chance that your house is being robbed.

TIRED OF CHINESE FOOD? NEXT TIME TRY "ROCKY'S PIZZA"!

FORTUNE COOKIE ADS GET READ! FOR A SPACE IN A COOKIE LIKE THIS ONE, CALL:
Business Biscuits Enterprises, Incorporated, 42 Main Street, City—555-9900

LEGALIZE ACUPUNCTURE!

Why bother to save for a rainy day? You only get soaked by inflation!

An apple a day could give you more pesticides than your body can tolerate.

THE GRASS IS ALWAYS GREENER . . . FOR THE PUSHER.

FORTUNE COOKIES THAT ARE RELEVANT

WRITTEN BY: DICK DE BARTOLO & DON EPSTEIN

CRIME DOES NOT PAY... INCOME TAXES!

BOYCOTT LETTUCE!

Please open another cookie. The Fortune you have reached is not in service at this time!

BE CAREFUL OF WHAT YOU TALK ABOUT! THE TEAPOT MAY BE BUGGED!

EATING THIS COOKIE CAN BE HAZARDOUS TO YOUR HEALTH. IT CONTAINS EMULSIFIED GLYCOL, HYDROGENATED BENSOMENICAINE, PLUS BTA AND BHA.

Walk softly and carry a big stick. It's the only way you won't get mugged.

LIVE LONGER! BREATHE LESS OF TODAY'S AIR!

BYE, BYE BLACKBIRD... AND ALL THE OTHER ENDANGERED SPECIES!

A DOG IN THE BUSH IS WORTH TWO ON THE SIDEWALK!

BABY SITTING

BERG'S-EYE VIEW DEPT.

THE LIGHTE

GROWING UP

JOB QUALIFICATIONS

Perfectly! And he's thoroughly familiar with all the new tax laws, too!

So are all the other applicants! What makes him "DOUBLY QUALIFIED"?!?

R SIDE OF...

ARTIST & WRITER: DAVE BERG

MODERN MORALITY

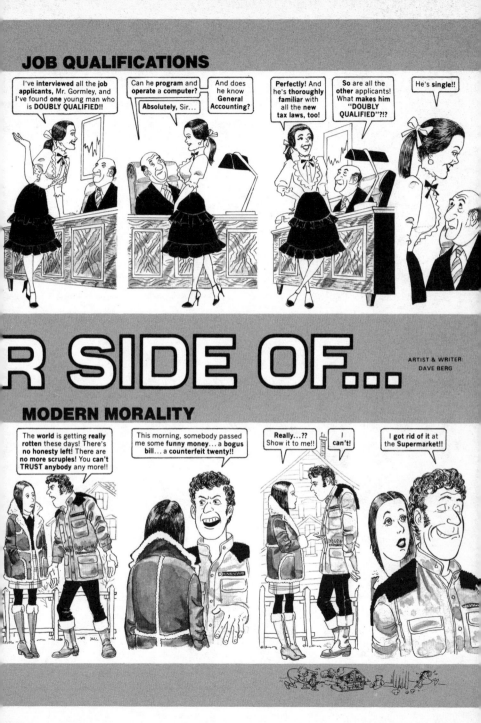

WISDOM

RELATIONSHIPS

STATUS CLOTHING

ECONOMICS

EATING OUT

CONCLUSIONS

SACRIFICES

FIREMEN

NAGGING

ASSUMPTIONS

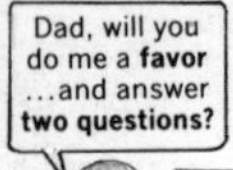

COPS

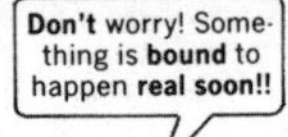

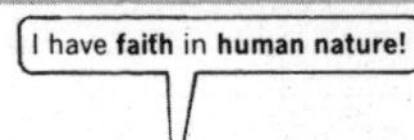

DON MARTIN DEPT.

ONE DAY ON A HIKE

Larry Bird's Bird and Michael J. Fox's Fox enjoying an afternoon in James Wood's Woods

SHEER NOUN-SENSE DEPT.

"What's in a name?" is the old questior sometimes asked. Well, it depends! As

THE NAME OF THE RICH

ARTIST: MORT DRUCKER

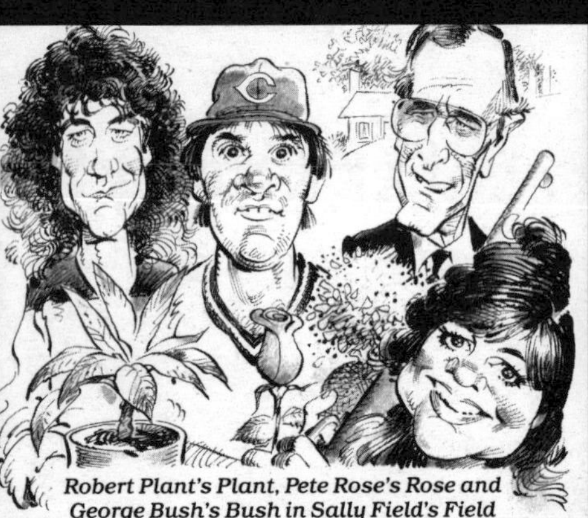
Robert Plant's Plant, Pete Rose's Rose and George Bush's Bush in Sally Field's Field

Tom Cruise's Cruise on Brian Ferry's Ferry

I HOPE TO BEG YOUR PARDON, SIR.
FORD
FORD

Gerald Ford's Ford meeting Harrison Ford's Ford

ou'll see in the following stupid scenes we've managed to come up with!

GAME AND FAMOUS

WRITER: J. PRETE

Kirstie Alley's Alley directly behind Darryl Hall's Hall

Judas Priest's Priest condemning Billy Idol's Idol

Rev. Moon's Moon in Elton John's John

Darryl Strawberry's Strawberry at the produce checkout line with Chuck Berry's Berry and Jack Lemmon's Lemon

HAVING A TRUTH PULLED DEPT.

A MAD LOOK AT SOME WIDELY HELD

ARTIST: HARVEY KURTZMA

MISCONCEPTION #29

If you don't feed your pets the right nationally advertised pet food they'll stop eating and die.

MISCONCEPTION #701

The price of a loaf of bread in 1953 is a topic of great interest among most younger people today.

MISCONCEPTION #180

Americans are sick and tired of deciding for themselves what they should or should not read.

MISCONCEPTION #82

The best way for a candidate to "win over" voters is to pre-empt their favorite television show with a half-hour political spiel.

MISCONCEPTION #425

People who wait in line and pay $5.00 for a theater seat would much rather listen to a neighbor's "running commentary" than watch the movie itself.

MISCONCEPTION #65

Students have plenty of time for extra homework—especially since their other four or five teachers don't believe in assigning any.

MISCONCEPTION #14

Attractive women can't resist obscene propositions from sweaty, overweight men in smelly T-shirts.

MISCONCEPTION #213

Elevators are intelligent beings and sense impatience when someone bangs their buttons repeatedly.

MISCONCEPTION #566

Nothing stimulates conversation like a mouthful of Novocain, dental instruments and fingers.

MISCONCEPTIONS

WRITER: MIKE SNIDER

MISCONCEPTION #31

Especially in high-speed traffic, using directional signals before making a lane change is unnecessary between experienced drivers.

MISCONCEPTION #7

There is nothing that shows your cleverness and wit better than a store-bought "gag sign" which five million people already own.

MISCONCEPTION #37

The proper greeting for a caller to a Customer Service line is 25 minutes of "The Hollywood Strings Play the Best of Barry Manilow."

JOKE AND DAGGER DEPT.

A WORD TO DEVICE DEPT.

You've read poems that glorify trees and Paul Revere and stuff like that. Let's face it—they're out of date. We're in the 1980s, and what deserves glorifying are the items that assist us every day and enrich our lives. You know, things like the Walkman, the blender and the VCR. Which is why Mad now presents

ODES TO APPLIANCES, GADGETS AND OTHER MODERN CONVENIENCES

ARTIST: GEORGE WOODBRIDGE IDEA: MARILYN ATKINS WRITER: FRANK JACOBS

O WALKMAN!

O Walkman! My Walkman!
I groove the tapes you play;
Your 'phones stay wrapped around my head
From dawn till end of day.

O Walkman! My Walkman!
You fill my life with sound;
Because of you, I now block out
All other sounds around.

O Walkman! My Walkman!
I hear you, there's no doubt;
I only wish I could have heard
The truck that wiped me out.

THE VCR

The VCR's a loyal pal,
A friend you truly care for,
Because it guarantees you'll see
The shows that you weren't there for;
Two thousand shows I've taped so far;
Each night I tape a new one;
Who knows, perhaps there'll come a day
I'll find the time to view one.

The Microwave

Blessings on thee, Microwave;
Countless minutes I now save;
Like a flash, you work with ease,
Roasting meats and melting cheese;
Turning out a cherry pie
In the twinkling of an eye;
Baking apples double-quick—
What's your secret? What's the trick?
Some great magic you possess;
What it is, I cannot guess;
Once my cooking spelled disaster;
Now it's just as bad—but faster.

The Nautilus

The Nautilus keeps me in trim
Just like a workout at the gym;
For half an hour, twice a day,
I strain to melt the flab away;
I lift and pull and stretch and push
To flatten gut and tighten tush;
You'll find this well-designed machine
Will make your body trim and lean;
It helps, of course, the makers say,
To use it ev'ry waking day;
But best of all, I should explain,
You'll love it if you're into pain.

BLENDER, BLENDER

Blender, blender, on my shelf,
Mixing foods all by yourself,
Pulverizing chicken chunks
Into spreads and dips and dunks.

Blender, blender, wondrous toy,
Source of gastronomic joy;
Chopping, churning while you work,
Like some wacko gone berserk.

Blender, blender, bladed friend,
Slicing carrots end to end;
Thanks to how you mush and mince,
I create a perfect blintz.

Blender, blender, fast and slick,
Making sauces rich and thick;
Faithfully, you'll serve me well
Till my diet's shot to hell.

PHONES

I think that I shall never own
A tool more handy than the phone;
A phone with which I keep in touch
With inlaws, old-time pals and such;
A phone that also sometimes rings
With calls from schmucks and dingalings;
A phone that bill collectors use
For giving me unwelcome news;
A phone with calls that airheads make
Who've dialed my number by mistake;
A phone I pick up half asleep
To hear some heavy-breathing creep;
On second thought, I've come to fear
There's less to phones than meets the ear;
In fact, with one more nuisance call
I may not own a phone at all.

BURY FUNNY DEPT.

DON EDWING LOO

WRITER AND ARTIST: DON EDWING

KS AT FUNERALS

DAILY BLAH BLAH
DECAPITATION VICTIM TO BE BURIED TODAY

Stop them!
Hey, come back here!
Anybody got a gun?
What should we do...??
I dunno! This neve happened before
CEMETERY

ING!
ING!
DING!
DING!

BLACK HUMOR
BLACK HUMOR

SPROING

B'DUM
B'DUM

BAM

You **lying rat bum!!** You told me you were **working**... and I find **THIS...!**
EDWING

A WORD TO THE GUISE DEPT.

There's a new book out called **Doublespeak,** which reveals how governments, advertisers and the media deceive us with twisted words and phrases. Like when hospitals refer to death as "terminal living." Or when a nuclear-plant explosion is called "energetic disassembly." Or when artificial leather is touted as "virgin vinyl." It's all part of a sneaky trend to make the bad seem good, the disgusting sound appealing, the deplorable seem acceptable! Yes, **Doublespeak** is on the rise, so we better prepare for the time...

WHEN TAKES

ARTIST: SERGIO ARAGON

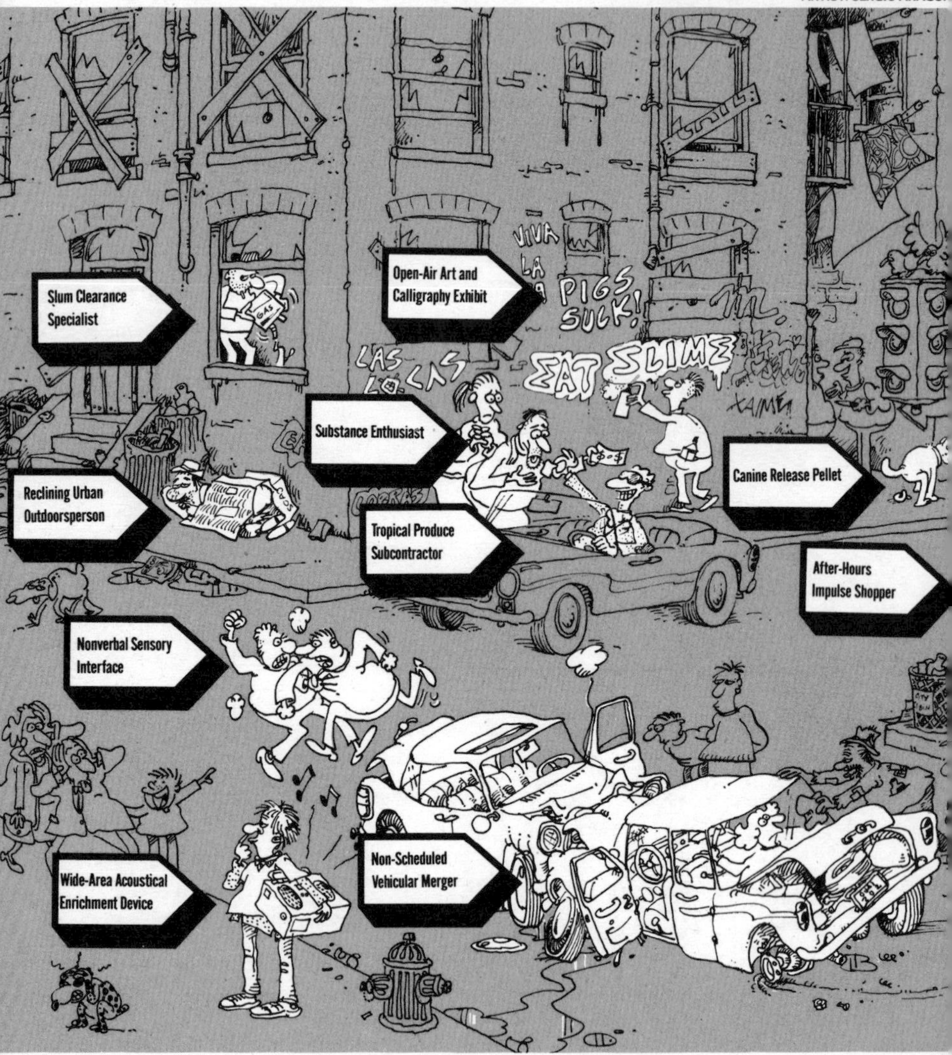

DOUBLESPEAK"
VER COMPLETELY

RITER: FRANK JACOBS

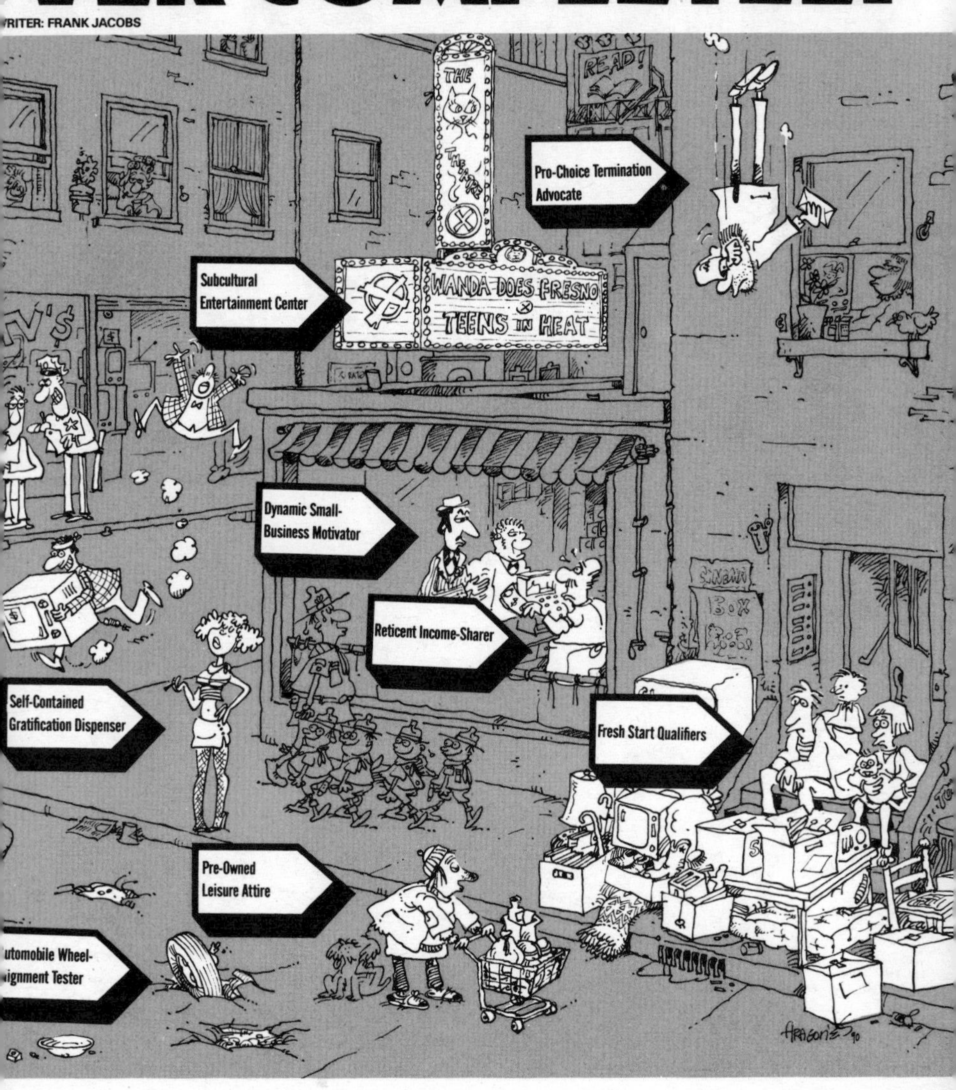

THEME SCHEME DEPT.

PATTERNS

7½	102	AlaP pf8.28	z50	104½	104½	104¼	104¼	− ¼
4⅛	19½	Alaska Inters	406	46¾	48¼	46½	47¾	+ ⅞
8⅞	20½	AlbetoC .32	33	27¾	27¾	26⅝	26⅝	−1¼
5	11¾	Albertsns .36	30	13⅛	13⅜	13⅛	13¼	+ ⅛
2⅞	17¾	AlcanAlu .80	21	20⅜	20½	20⅜	20⅜	
8⅜	11¼	AlcoStand .34	49	11½	11½	11⅛	11⅜	− ⅛
8	49¼	Alcon Lab .26	44	66¾	67	65¾	66¾	− ⅛
2¾	12¼	Alexndrs .30e	99	13⅜	13⅜	12⅞	13	− ⅜
4⅞	11⅛	AllALfe .24e	36	12¾	13	12¾	13	+ ⅛
4⅞	10⅛	Alleg Cp .20e	7	10½	10⅝	10½	10⅝	+ ⅛
8⅞	18¾	AllegLudlm 1	30	28	28	27⅝	27⅞	− ⅛
0⅞	38	AllegLud pf 3	10	40⅝	40¾	40½	40⅝	
3¾	20⅜	AllegPw 1.40	136	20¾	20¾	20⅝	20⅝	− ⅛
0½	16¼	AllenGp 1.04t	50	23⅝	23⅞	23½	23¾	− ⅛
6¾	27¾	Allied Ch 1.20	49	30	30	29¼	29½	− ½
5⅝	39½	Alld Main .45	46	39¼	39½	38⅞	39½	
2½	18¼	AlldMills .75	6	19¾	19¾	19¼	19¼	− ¾
5¼	18	Allied Pd .68	6	18⅜	18⅜	18⅛	18⅛	− ½
6¾	44	AlliedPd pf 3	4	46	46	46	46	
7	30½	AlliedStr 1.40	18	34¼	34½	34¼	34½	+ ¼
8½	54	AlliedStr pf 4	z130	57	58	57	58	− ½
8⅜	4⅜	Allied Super	31	4⅝	4¾	4⅝	4¾	+ ⅛
5⅜	11½	AllisChal .20e	42	11¾	11¾	11½	11⅝	
2⅜	19¼	AllrgtAut .48	38	19½	19½	19	19	− ¾
9¼	16¼	AlphaPrt Ind	3	16¼	16¼	16⅛	16⅛	− ⅛
6⅛	38⅞	Alcoa 1.80	67	50	50⅛	49⅝	49⅝	− ⅜
9⅜	24¾	AmalSug 1.60	5	25	25	24¾	24¾	− ½
8¼	12⅞	AMBAC .50	45	16⅜	16⅜	16	16	− ⅛
0¾	21¼	Amer Es 1.20	14	27½	27½	27¼	27½	+ ¼
1¼	41	Am Es pf2.60	7	46½	46¾	46½	46¾	− ¼

27⅞	24⅞	Cencoinst
38¾	24¾	Centex C
24⅞	21¾	CenHud
28¼	22¾	CenIllLt
20⅛	16½	CenIlPS
24⅞	19⅝	CenLaE
18⅞	17	CenMPw
49⅜	40½	CenSoWt
30¾	23¾	Cent Soy
21⅝	17¼	CenTelUt
17¾	12⅞	CerroCp
61¼	42⅝	Cert-teed
35	25	CessnaAi
4⅞	2⅞	Chadbrn
30½	20⅞	ChampInt
31½	23	Chml pf1
53	43½	ChampS
36⅜	29	Charter
...	...	ChaseFd
60⅝	52	ChaseMar
57½	46½	ChaseT 3
18⅛	12⅝	Chelsea
28½	21	Chemetrn
59½	49	ChemNY
36¾	30⅛	ChesVa 1
59¾	46⅜	Ches O 2
84	56⅜	Chesbgh
14	9⅜	ChiMilw
26¼	17¼	ChiMilw

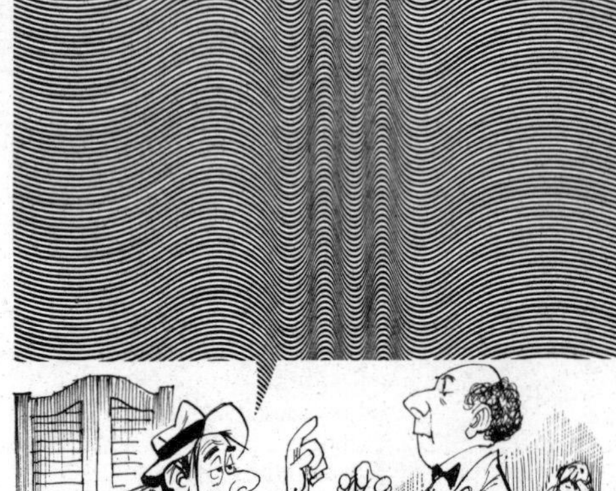

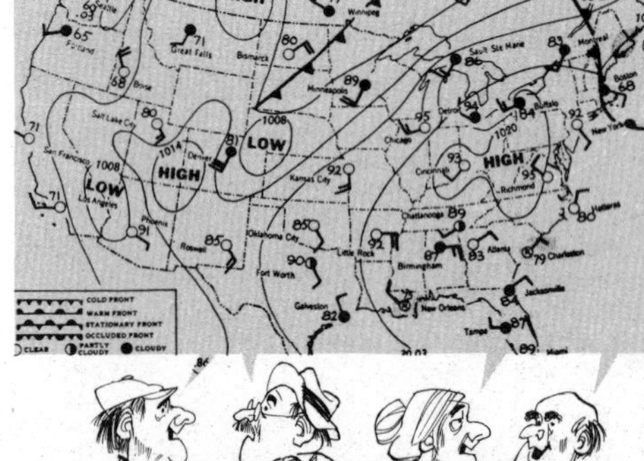

BRING BACK POTRZEBIE

OF SPEECH

ARTIST: BOB CLARKE
IDEA BY MAX BRANDEL

GUIDED MUSCLES DEPT.

Today, thousands of health-conscious people are not only jogging, but submitting their bodies to all kinds of punishment in Health Clubs across the country equipped with Nautilus exercise machines. Now, as we see it, the real

SPECIALIZED NAU
FOR PRACTICAL EVE

ARTIST: AL JAFFEE

A Neck-Stretching Machine

To develop your neck muscles, thereby enabling you to extend your head great distances in different directions...

...for cheating on school exams, aptitude tests, etc.

A Shoulder-Building Machine

To strengthen shoulder muscles so that you will be able to carry enormous weights over long periods of time...

...for all you music lovers who get your kicks out of forcing your preference in music on helpless passersby.

-roblem with Nautilus machines is that outside of making look like a poor man's Arnold Schwarzenegger, they've got very little practical value. Which is why we'd like to offer any interested entrepreneur our suggestions for

TILUS MACHINES RYDAY ACTIVITIES

/RITER: LARRY SIEGEL

A Wrist-Conditioning Machine

To recondition and strengthen your weak, stiff wrists so they will be able to function with hair-trigger speed...

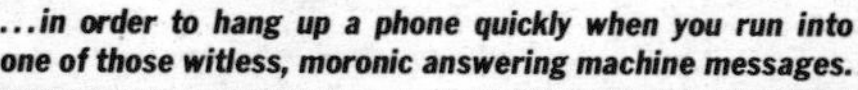

...in order to hang up a phone quickly when you run into one of those witless, moronic answering machine messages.

A Back-Strengthening Machine

To harden your neck, buttocks and thigh muscles...

...so you'll survive being dragged away from demonstrations.

A Contortion-Training Machine

To make your body supple and loose in order to enable it to twist into positions it has never been in before...

...for making out in a BMW with a 5-speed stick shift.

A Steel Punching Bag

To develop tremendous strength in hands and knuckles...

...for punching out those broken pay telephones and video games and cigarette machines that never return your money.

An Over-All Body-Building Machine

To build up your entire body for the vital "Decathlon of Life"...

...in order to run fast enough to escape nuclear plant leakages, to leap high enough to clear toxic waste dumps, to swim strongly enough to out-distance oil slicks and 7 other catastrophic events too horrible and disgusting to mention.

DON MARTIN DEPT.

ONE DAY IN A GARAGE

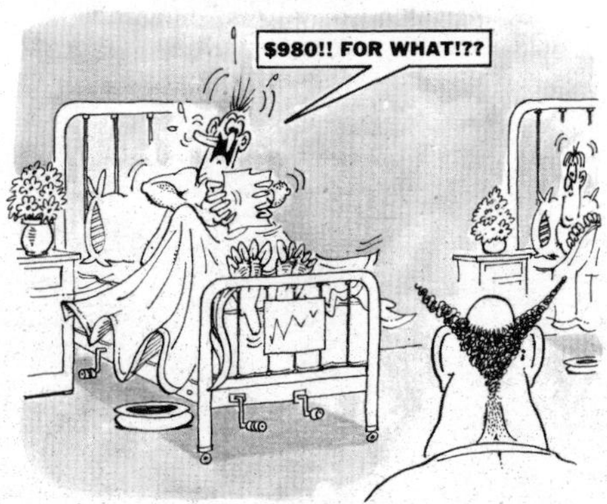

FROM BAD TO VOICE DEPT.

What's the newest thing on the science front? White bread...?! Boy, are you out of touch! No, it's the "Voice Synthesizer," a miniature computer chip that "talks." So far, we already have clocks that "speak" the time,

WHAT IT WILL BE LIKE WH

ARTIST: PAUL COKER

Can I **help** you?
Yes! I'd like to withdraw **two hundred dollars** from my **account!**
Two hundred? What are you going to do with **that** kind of money?
Hey... that's **MY business!** It's **MY MONEY!!**
Don't get wise with **me!!** It only takes **one computer error** to **wipe out** an **entire account!**

C'mon folks! **One** at a **time!!**

Hey, **stupid!** What kind of a word is **"teh"?** Do you mean **"the"?!** Say **yes,** and I'll **correct** it for you!

You want **me** to copy some **JOKE SHEET?!?** It's bad enough you **wrote it** on **company time!** Let's not use the **company machine** and the **company's paper** to circulate it!

What kind of **picture** is **this?!?** She's got a **stupid smile** on her face, and the **background** is **much too busy!** C'mon, gi'me a **break!!**

When you **finish drinking** that soda, will you make sure you **dispose** of the can **properly!?** This city is **filthy enough** without any **MORE** litter...!!

and autos that "tell" when something is about to go wrong mechanically. How long will it be before just about everything has a voice? Oh, just about the time it will take you to read this article which we've titled:

EN EVERY DEVICE "TALKS"

WRITER: DICK DE BARTOLO

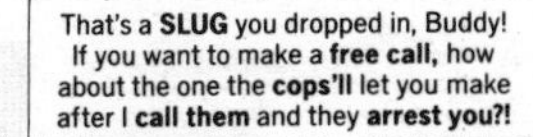

That's a **SLUG** you dropped in, Buddy! If you want to make a **free call,** how about the one the **cops'll** let you make after I **call them** and they **arrest you?!**

Hey! Someone get the guy who owns this **car** and tell him he's only got **five minutes left...!!**

Boy, you're gonna be **some sick kid** if you eat all this **junk food!** Ever hear of **vegetables? Salads? Cereals? Huh??**
CHIPS 95
CHIPS

I'm just about out of **milk,** and I'm really low on **eggs,** and I can use—

That's your **third cup!!** If **I** were **you,** I'd make sure I stopped in the **bathroom** before I started my hour trip to work!!

Hey, **Idiot**... why do it the **slow, painful way** with **cigarettes...?!** Why not just run in front of a **bus** and get it over with **quickly?!**

A SERVING OF SPARE FIBS DEPT.

We all do idiotic, embarrassing things. Then we try to blab our way out with excuses tha are even more idiotic. Why? Because when you wait till the last minute, you concoct lous

MAD'S ALIBIS FO

TO POLICE

ARTIST: JACK DAVIS WRITER: TOM KOCH

TO COACHES

TO EMPLOYERS

ies! So we say, "Be prepared!" Memorize some good alibis! But don't be caught reading this article—because we won't be able to help you! *That* kind of goof-up is not covered in...

R ALL OCCASIONS

TO PARENTS

There was no way I could have known it was after curfew because a mugger took my watch!
I purposely left my clothes on the floor to help insulate the room and cut your heating bill.
A prowler must have broken in and left all those copies of *Penthouse* on my closet floor.
SCARSDALE
56
GO GIANTS
13

TO SWEETHEARTS

I know we made a commitment to each other, and all the rest of the people I date respect that.
Normally I wouldn't ask you to pay, but my credit's so good at most places I don't carry cash.
The lipstick stains are from a female paramedic who goes around saving lives with free demonstrations of artificial respiration.

TO TEACHERS

I did not write that term paper for fear it would be so good I'd set a standard that I couldn't live up to.
I took yesterday off because I thought nobody cared. But now that I know you missed me, it was completely worth it.
That excuse note doesn't look like my mother's handwriting because she's sick in bed with exactly the same thing I had.
Teecher

ADS BACKWARDS DEPT.

Back in 1968 (MAD #116), we published some "Ads We Never Got To See" ... a collection of ill-fated advertising campaigns that sounded good when they were first created, but upon reflection certainly

MORE ADS WE N

Try the ALL-NEW
WeightWatchers
DIET PROGRAM!
you have nothing to lose
...and everything to gain!

The ALL-NEW
Space Age
ZENITH
HEARING
AID
it's something
to shout about

LEARN TO DRIVE
in
ONE DAY
WITH
FENWICK
AUTO SCHOOL'S
8-HOUR CRASH COURSE
IN DRIVING!

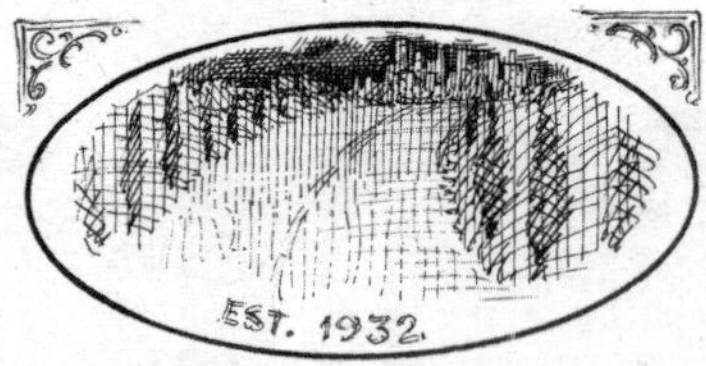

idn't say what the advertisers intended to say. Vell, it's taken sixteen years for the laughter to die down. And now that everyone's had a chance to catch his breath, we're ready to go again with...

VER GOT TO SEE

ARTIST: HARRY NORTH WRITER: DICK DE BARTOLO

why not pick your own nose?
THE CRANSTON COSMETIC SURGERY CLINIC
NEW TRAVEL SIZE
Pepto-Bismol
TABLETS
For people on the go!
fly
EASTERN
It's the American way!

PREPARATION H

For temporary hemorrhoid relief,
it leaves all the others behind!

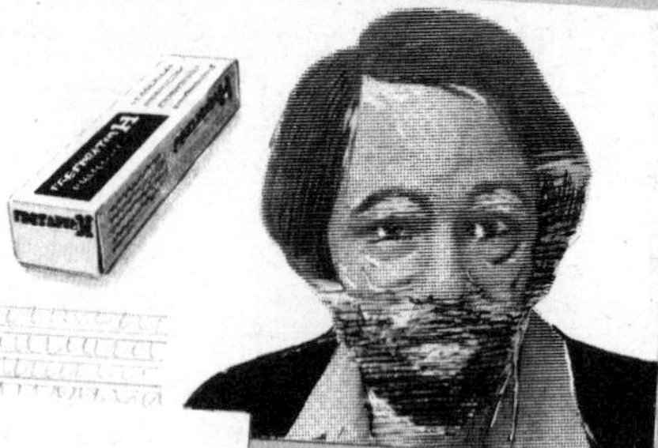

Brillo

SOAP PADS
We're always working to improve
them and we've just started
to scratch the surface!

Let our cheerful drivers take you for a ride!

DON MARTIN DEPT.

ONE NIGHT IN THE ACME RITZ CENTRAL ARMS WALDORF PLAZA STATLER HILTON GRAND HOTEL

TERMINAL ILLNESS DEPT.

We're told that the most miraculous thing about computers is their ability to store and feed back millions of bits of information. But in MAD's opinion, that's not the most miraculous thing about computers. The real miracle is that not one of the millions of facts they have stored away is the correct spelling

IF COMPUTERS A

...why do they assume you want to receive 800 identical copies of the same mail order catalogue?

...why do they spread the word that you're responsible for all of the 1983 and 1984 parking tickets issued to a car that you sold in 1981?

...why does the increasing amount of information they spew out to TV weathermen only make the forecasts more inaccurate?

...how come they're always telling you that you're making an error, but they can never tell you what it is?

...what is their logic in letting 14,000 murders go unsolved while they devote full time to nailing you on some old traffic warrant?

...why do they blithely pass along a ridiculous meter reading that makes your monthly electric bill higher than the one for Yankee Stadium?

of our name, or our accurate address, or a single smidgeon of data about us that is completely right! As each of us wastes hours and hours trying to correct the garble spewed out by some crazed silicon chip, we are bound to wonder how that much stupidity can be produced with such unfailing regularity...

RE SO BRILLIANT...

ARTIST: GEORGE WOODBRIDGE WRITER: TOM KOCH

...why can't they report your correct wages to the I.R.S., especially when it's a known fact that the I.R.S. will always believe a computer and assume the taxpayer is lying?

...why can't they find someone to write a computer instruction manual who knows how to put together a simple sentence?

...why do they invariably select the phone numbers of the elderly, the unmarried and the childless to receive their annoying calls about diaper service?

...how do they figure that your bank balance could have dropped from $1,854 to $18.54 during a month you didn't make any withdrawals?

...why do they insist that "JOHNSMITH" is all one word, and must be alphabetized under "J" until its poor owner gets around to acquiring a first name?

...why do companies that install them immediately have to hire lots of extra employees just to correct computer errors?

UP-CHUCKLES DEPT.

A MAD LOOK AT AMUSEM

ENT PARKS

ARTIST & WRITER: SERGIO ARAGONES

1
PENNY
ARCA
TONG!
BOX

2
PENNY
ARCA
TING!
BOX

1
THE PULPO

2

1
HOUSE OF MIRRORS

2

3

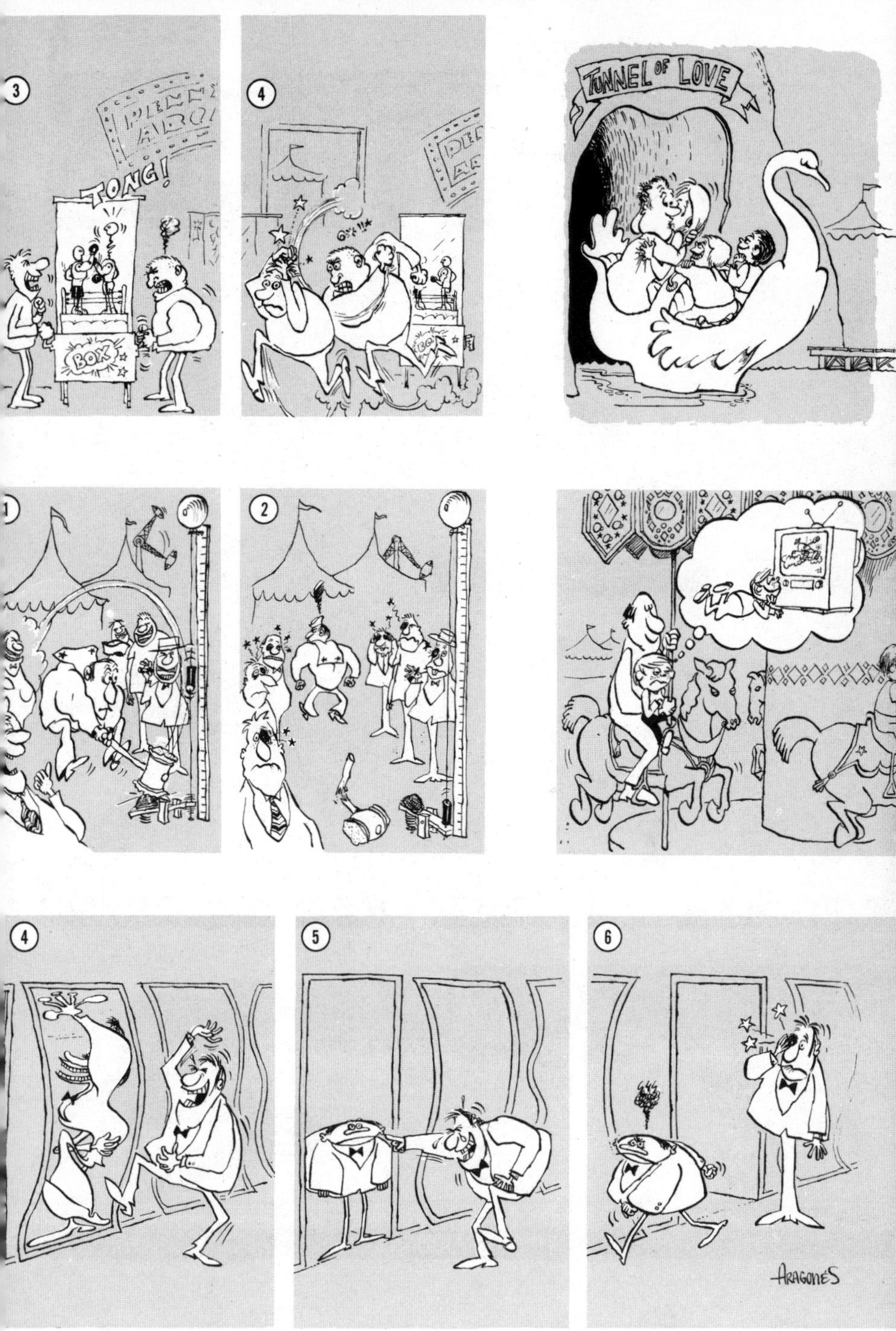

3
TONG!
BOX
4
TUNNEL OF LOVE
1
2
4
5
6
ARAGONES

TIPS FOR ZIPS DEPT.

PASTIMES

TREE TUG-OF-WAR

DRIP-DRIP SING-A-LONG

ARM WRESTLING WITH IRONING BOARD

TWISTER-DODGING

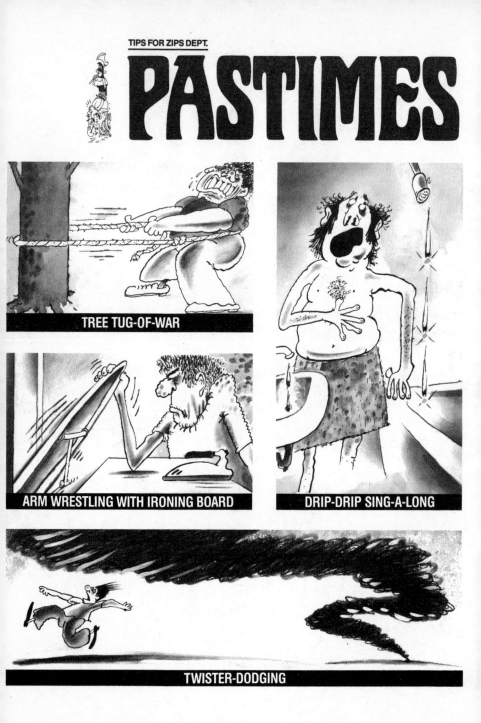

for NERDS

WRITER AND ARTIST: PAUL PETER PORGES

FULL-BODY APPLE-DUNKING

ONE MAN TOUCH-FOOTBALL

UNICYCLE TO A DRIVE-IN MOVIE

JOKE AND DAGGER DEPT.

PLANE NONSENSE DEPT.
The MAD People Watcher's Guide to an Airport
ARTIST: TOM BUNK
WRITER: MIKE SNIDER
Blissfully unaware that she's just **erased** 200 Christmas reservations from the computer.
About to become **statistic** on **police blotter** when she tells **"Mongo"** he's spent an **hour** on the **wrong line.**
DEPARTURES
CHANGE
JAPAN AIR LINES
Promised he'd flush a **"frozen surprise"** over his friend Timmy's house after takeoff.
Isn't a terrorist; just gets off on having people **think** he is.
Is a terrorist, and worried **sick** about guy in turban!
RAVIOLI the MAGICIAN

BOARDING GATE B
Prepared to argue about the definition of "carry-on" for **hours**, if necessary!
Building up a **4-hour supply** of **nicotine** in **bloodstream** before boarding.
NO SMOKING ON AIRCRAFT!
Petrified of flying; now back in the "friendly skies" after trying to deal with **Amtrak!**
Desperately hoping his **wife** doesn't show up to see him off.
Check in
X-RAYS
Takes **"Foo-Foo"** everywhere she flies; now going to **clinic** for **doggie-tranquilizer addiction!**
Just spent **3 hours** driving to airport and finding parking space for a **30-minute shuttle flight.**
NYACK ... OR BUST
Pretending to be engrossed in article on **Bob Saget** so dork in next seat doesn't start up a conversation.
Actually only wants to **read** the Bob Saget piece after she's **done!**
BRAU
THANK YOU
Spent **years** perfecting his "You undertipped me" sneer and grunt.
WELCOME TO NEW YORK
MOSTLY MOZART
HOMELESS
HUNGRY
THIRSTY
GREEDY

I AM
AERO ФЛОТ
ICELAND AIR
HAWAII AIR
VATICAN AIR
First in his class at the APEX 10-minute Airport Security Training School!
Has to break Carl Lewis's 1988 Olympic Record to make connecting flight leaving from Terminal D.
International Arrivals
INT. ARRIVALS
Feeling every bit as stupid as they look doing this!
ON STRIKE
WONG
WONG
GODOT
EDDYE
I ♥ NY
Wondering if that 10 minutes alone in the plane's restroom puts him in the "Mile High Club."
Followed wrong colored line on floor 3 days ago; still looking for son-in-law picking her up.
Have formed impromptu betting pool over which continent their luggage wound up on.
EGYPT AIR
Would like to get his hands on the creep who thought up wheels on suitcases.
Pretty sure he remembered to tighten those engine bolts on that last DC-10.
T. BUNK

DICK DePT.

OK, we have truth in advertising, so now how about some...

TRUTH IN

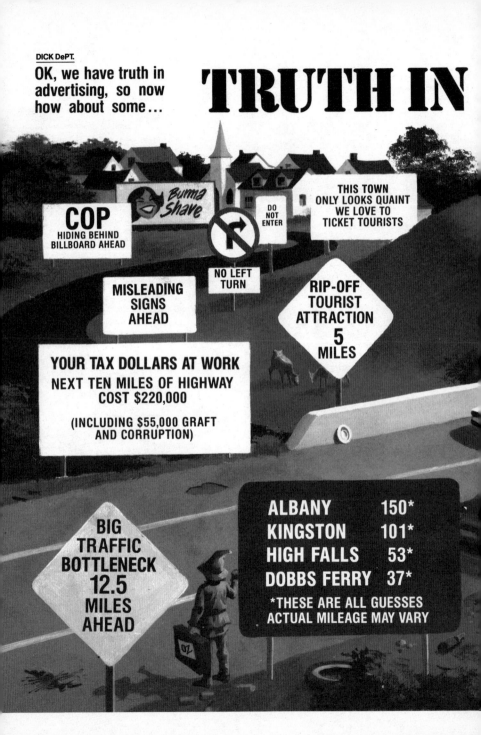

ROAD SIGNS

ARTIST: BOB CLARKE
WRITER: DICK DE BARTOLO

STOP-PAY TOLL

REAL SLOW TOLL COLLECTOR

AVERAGE SPEED TOLL COLLECTOR

SUPER FAST TOLL COLLECTOR

BUT COUNT YOUR CHANGE

FILTHY RESTROOMS
BROKEN PAY PHONES
INEDIBLE FOOD
NEXT EXIT

GET OUT MAP
LAST HELPFUL SIGN
FOR NEXT 20 MILES
AHEAD

CONSTRUCTION
MEN
GOOFING OFF

SO-SO
SCENIC
VIEW
NEXT
RIGHT

FALLING
ROCK
ZONE

ROOMMATES

BERG'S-EYE VIEW DEPT.

THE LIGHTE

THE ECONOMY

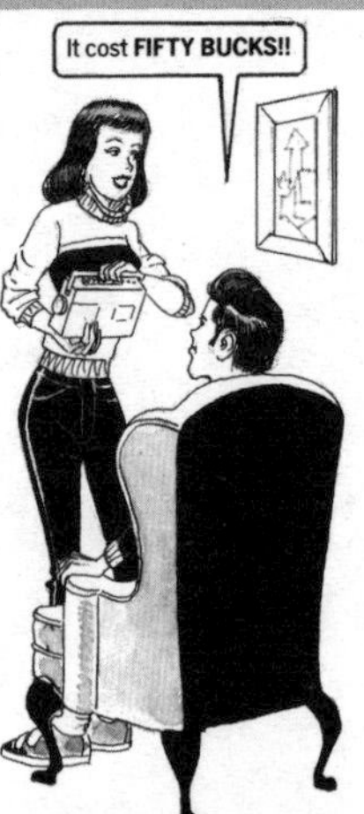

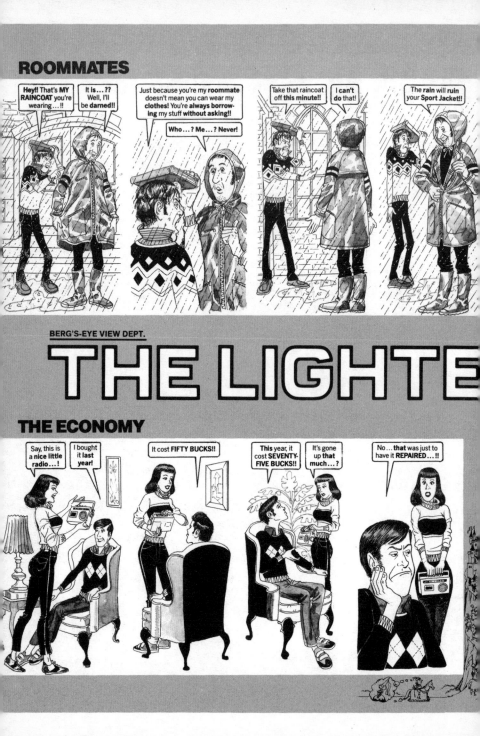

PANHANDLING

R SIDE OF...

ARTIST & WRITER: DAVE BERG

ADVICE

FORTUNE TELLING

BIRTHDAYS

STRANGE BEHAVIO

POLITICS

BREAKING UP

NAMES

CLOTHING

PETS

THE JOB

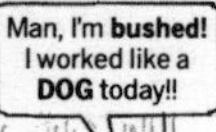

WHEELS

BS.A.T. DEPT.

Thinking about what career to get into? Wondering whether or not you'll fit in? Well, here's the first in a series of tests designed to help you choose your future line of work. Mainly, discover your true abilities by taking...

MAD'S APTITUDE TEST NUMBER ONE

WILL YOU MAKE A GOOD DOCTOR?

1. You are a surgeon who is operating on another doctor's patient. Through a mix-up of X-rays, you remove the patient's kidneys instead of his appendix. Who should take responsibility?
   A. You, if you have good malpractice coverage.
   B. The other doctor, if you have a sharp lawyer.
   C. The hospital, if both of you have sharp lawyers.
   D. Any of the above.

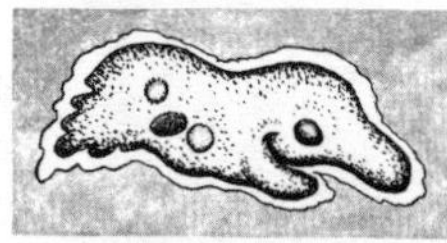

2. You should be able to tell that the above is:
   A. A white blood cell.
   B. A streptococcus germ.
   C. The 4th green at Rolling Hills Golf Course.
   D. All of the above.

3. Complete this sentence: You should study to be a specialist, because _ .
   A. Unlike GPs, you don't have to mess with low income-producing ailments such as head colds and sore throats.
   B. A fancy title like cardiologist or dermatologist by itself jacks up your income 100%.
   C. Only another specialist in your exact same field can tell when you botch up a diagnosis.
   D. All of the above.

4. Complete this sentence. You should study to be a GP, because ______ .
   A. You can refer cases to a specialist and split his fee.
   B. You get to try out a lot more new and different fun drugs and see what happens.
   C. You can collect more of those little $20 and $30 office visits in pocketable tax-free cash.
   D. All of the above.

5. While being examined in his doctor's office, a patient goes into shock. The most probable cause is:
   A. The doctor kept him sitting only five minutes in the waiting room.
   B. The doctor is giving advice to another patient by phone, instead of making him come into the office.
   C. The doctor wrote out a prescription that was totally legible.
   D. All of the above.

6. Complete this sentence: A proper "Bedside Manner" is __________ .
   A. Seeming concerned about a patient's ailment while all the time trying to figure out if the I.R.S. will allow the business deduction you took for both your Cadillac and souped-up Alfa Romeo.
   B. Asking friendly questions about a patient's job in order to get a line on his income bracket so you can take him for the maximum fee he can stand.
   C. Making a hospital patient believe that the 30 seconds of chitchat you spend with him each day is evidence of your deep personal concern.
   D. Any of the above.

7. When a doctor runs a series of tests, he can be reasonably certain that they:
   A. Will be inconclusive.
   B. Are unnecessary.
   C. Will cost the patient a minimum of $100 in lab fees.
   D. All of the above.

8. As a doctor, it will be helpful for you to be connected with a top-rated hospital. Why?
   A. The comfy Doctor's Lounge is a great place to hide out in when you're ducking those pesky emergency calls.
   B. Just the mention of the hospital's name can often net you a 50% increase in the size of your fee.
   C. Walking through the halls in a white coat and a stethoscope around your neck and hearing yourself being paged is a groovy ego trip.
   D. All of the above.

9. 

   As a doctor, you discover this auto crash victim on the highway. Your first concern is to:
   A. Do nothing until you have proof of his ability to pay.
   B. Do nothing until he signs a release stating you won't be sued for malpractice.
   C. Tell him to drink plenty of liquids and call your nurse for an appointment.
   D. Any of the above.

10. When a doctor is unable to pinpoint an ailment, which of these cop-outs is most effective?
   A. "I'd explain what you've got, but it's so technical you wouldn't understand it."
   B. "It's too early to tell."
   C. "It looks like nothing, but if it's still bothering you next week, call up for another appointment."
   D. Any of the above.

SCORING

If you answered "D." to all the questions, you have the ability to make a fine Doctor.

ARTIST: GEORGE WOODBRIDGE
WRITER: FRANK JACOBS

KIDDIE CUM LAUDE DEPT.

Recently, a West Coast minister wrote a best-selling book entitled *All I Really Need to Know I Learned in Kindergarten*. At MAD our immediate response was, "What took you so long, Reverend?" We've always known that kindergarten teaches kids how to share, how to pick up their toys, and how to operate heavy machinery. But most kids learn other skills *long* before age five—how to brown nose, how avoid blame and how to play dumb! Just think back and surely you'll agree with us that...

ALL YOU NEED TO KNOW YOU LEARNED IN NURSERY SCHOOL

ARTIST: PAUL COKER WRITER: TOM KOCH

If you think you may mess things up, be sure there's someone else handy to blame it on.

Never volunteer for anything unless you're positive someone else will get picked.

Only guys with empty sand pails say they'll stop throwing sand in your face if you'll stop throwing it in theirs.

Don't waste time crying until there's somebody important around to hear you.

The only good time to start a fight is when the other person isn't ready.

If you never do anything, you can't get chewed out for doing part of it wrong.

Being offered a cookie by somebody who doesn't even like you usually means it's a lousy cookie.

After you break something, be sure you're not still there when someone finds out.

Never do your best, or they'll expect you to be that good every time.

MEDIA-MORPHOSIS DEPT.

We've had it! We're fed up! We're STEAMED at the way Hollywood keeps ripping off comic strip
Batman, Superman, Dick Tracy, Popeye and plenty of others have been turned into stinky movies b

IF Famou

WERE M

COMIC

THE GODFATHER **By Charles Schulz**

PSYCHO **By Cathy Guisewite**

roducers who can't think up original ideas of their own. MAD thinks turnabout is fair play! It's bout time the comic strip business did some ripping off of their own! Yeah!! Just imagine…

Movies

DE INTO

STRIPS

ARTIST AND WRITER: RUSS COOPER

HONEY, I SHRUNK THE KIDS By Bill Watterson

LEAN ON ME By Garry Trudeau

CRIES AND WHISPERS By Jim Davis

TAXI DRIVER By Bil Keane

"Hey Daddy, are you gonna eat that piece of pie, huh, Daddy? Daddy?... Daddy?"

GODZILLA By Jim Unger

GREAT BALLS OF FIRE By Dean Young & Stan Drake

DANGEROUS LIAISONS By The Archie Comics Group

A NIGHTMARE ON ELM STREET By Johnny Hart

PLATOON By Berke Breathed

THROW MOMMA FROM THE TRAIN By Mell Lazarus

FAUX PAS FOR THE COURSE DEPT.

Do you stick your foot in your mouth so often that you know the shoe size of your face? Ar

A MAD GUIDE TO SOCIAL

How Not to Go fr

ARTIST: BOB JONES

your manners so awful that even Morton Downey Jr. avoids you? Then this course is for you! It's

BEHAVIOR

m Bad to Worse!

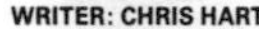
WRITER: CHRIS HART

If they say this...
Whatever you do, don't say this...
But if you do, and they say this...
You're really in the dumper if you say this...
This comes from a secret family recipe.
Tastes like the school cafeteria learned your secret!
If you're going to say something, say something positive!
Well, I sure am glad the portions are small!

If they say this...
Whatever you do, don't say this...
But if you do, and they say this...
You're really in the dumper if you say this...
Give me one good reason why I should raise your allowance.
So I can afford to stop stealing from your wallet!
You're going to pay back every cent!
That depends on how much I get for mom's jewelry!

If they say this...
Whatever you do, don't say this...
But if you do, and they say this...
You're really in the dumper if you say this...
Are you two going to study for your test?
How much do you have to study for a pregnancy test?
You mean you got my daughter pregnant?!
Hey, it's either me or the football team!

DON MARTIN DEPT.

ONE DAY DURING A CAVALRY ATTACK

WASH BORED GAMES DEPT.

Do you remember when your family would go on those long boring car trips? And do you remember how your Mother would try to keep you kids entertained with "Auto Bingo"... that stupid little game with the cows and stop signs, etc.? Well, what we have here is a similar game for another boring activity kids have to do with their parents. Here's

LAUNDROMAT BINGO

ARTIST: BOB CLARKE WRITER: RURIK TYLER

OVER-LOADED MACHINE

TANGLED CARTS

ADVICE-SEEKER

TV ADDICT

TANGLED CLOTHES

QUARTER CHASER

QUARTER EATER

SHRUNKEN CLOTHES

FIGHT OVER DRYER

DISGUSTING CHILD

MISSING CHILD

OLD MACHINES

NEW MACHINES

CLOTHES-FOLDER

FREE SPACE

RUG WASHER

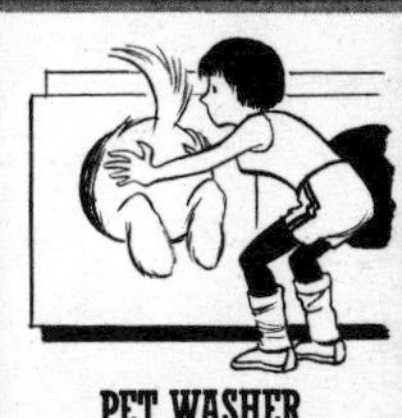

PET WASHER

LEAKS

LOST SOCK

OVERFLOWING GARBAGE CAN

MISSPELLED SIGN

WATERBUG

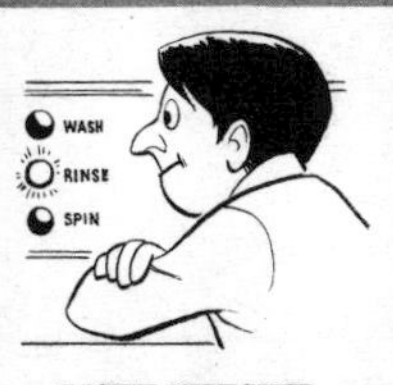

LIGHT WATCHER

LAST MINUTE WASHER

WET SPOT

ALL JAFFEE DEPT.

MAD MINI-MOVIES Featuring The Fickle Finger Of Fate

ARTIST & WRITER: AL JAFFEE

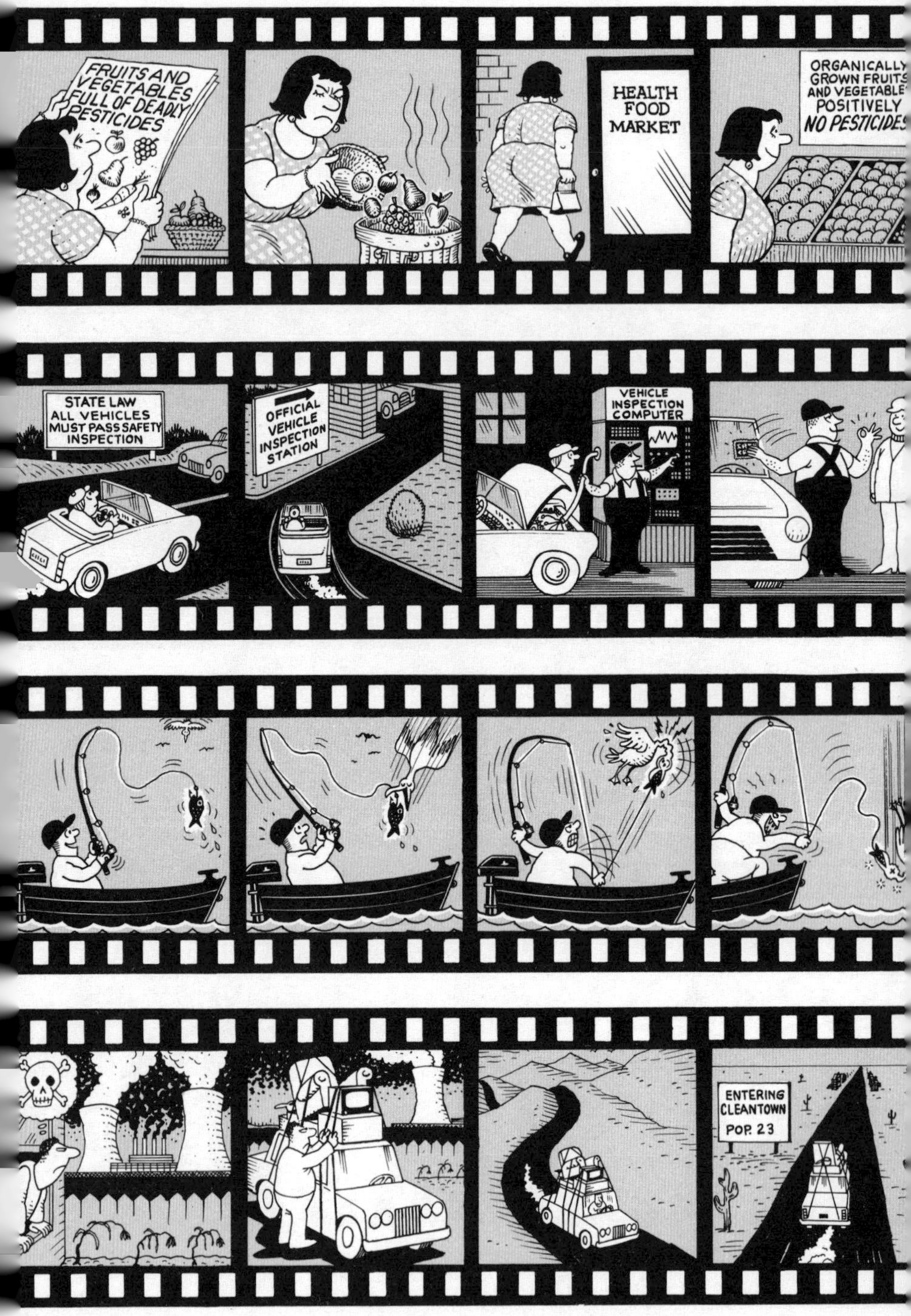

FRUITS AND VEGETABLES FULL OF DEADLY PESTICIDES

HEALTH FOOD MARKET

ORGANICALLY GROWN FRUITS AND VEGETABLES POSITIVELY NO PESTICIDES

STATE LAW ALL VEHICLES MUST PASS SAFETY INSPECTION

OFFICIAL VEHICLE INSPECTION STATION

VEHICLE INSPECTION COMPUTER

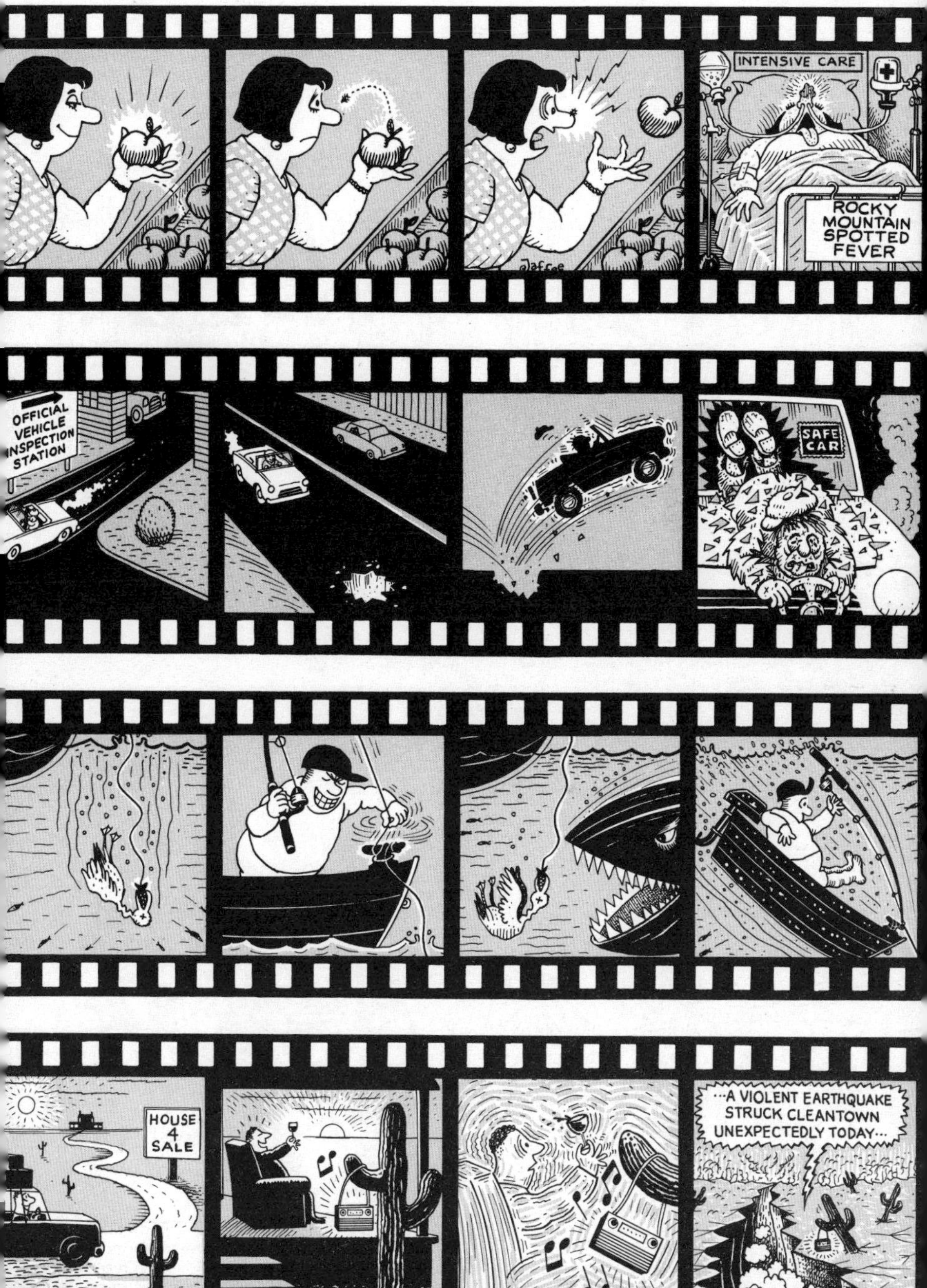

INTENSIVE CARE
ROCKY MOUNTAIN SPOTTED FEVER

OFFICIAL VEHICLE INSPECTION STATION
SAFE CAR

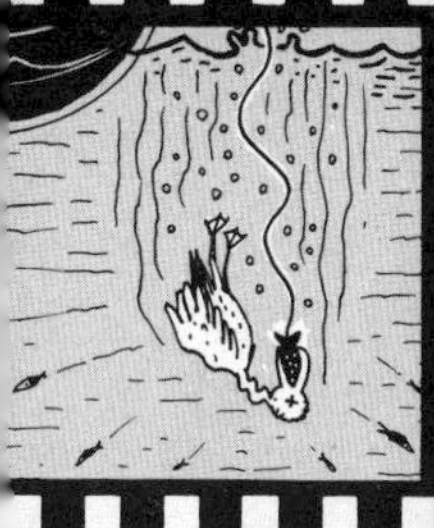

Cassandra was given the gift of prophecy because of her looks, but in an ironic twist, no one believed anything that came out of her mouth.

Milli Vanilli was given the gifts of record contracts and Grammys because of their looks, but in an ironic twist, no one will ever again believe anything that comes out of their mouths.

PARALLEL BARBS DEPT.

Thousands of years ago, the ancient Greeks and Romans worshipped a plethora of goddesses and gods which they believed to be all powerful and omnipotent. Of course, this was just mindless superstition. Modern civilization has taught us that only rock stars are all powerful and omnipotent! Still, from Mars to Martika, from Janus to Janet Jackson, these bigger than life figures have been revered and idolized for centuries. So, join us now, won't you? as MAD exposes...

THE STARTLING ANCIENT MYTHO

ARTIST: RICK TULKA

Hephaestus was hailed for being the god of fire. Despite being short, unattractive and misshapen, he somehow managed to wed the most beautiful goddess in Olympia.

Billy Joel is hailed for "We Didn't Start the Fire." Despite being short, unattractive and misshapen, he somehow managed to wed Chrisy Brinkley, the most beautiful goddess in the swimsuit issue.

The Phoenix was a mysterious animal who hid in a secret location every 500 years, set itself on fire and reemerged from its ashes with a new appearance.

Michael Jackson is a mysterious animal who hides in secret locations and releases an album every five years. He's been known to set himself on fire, and he frequently reemerges with a new appearance.

SIMILARITIES BETWEEN LOGY & MODERN ROCK

WRITER: DESMOND DEVLIN

Medusa was a frightening monster in ancient Greece, with grotesque, slimy snakes instead of hair. No living thing could look directly at her face without being turned into stone.

Prince is a frightening monster at PMRC headquarters, with grotesque, slimy hair. No living thing can look directly at his face without being turned into a punching bag by his private goon squad.

Midas, a minor king, received a priceless gift—anything he touched turned into gold. He quickly became rich with his new talent, but as soon as he got his power, he lost it. His ears were changed into those of an ass, and although he tried to hide under his hat, his shame was obvious to everyone.

2 Live Crew, a minor rap group, received a priceless gift—prosecutors craving headlines. They quickly became rich, but as soon as they got their audience, they lost it. Fans with ears thought the group asses, and while they tried to hide behind the First Amendment, their lack of talent was obvious to everyone.

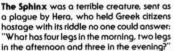

The Sphinx was a terrible creature, sent as a plague by Hera, who held Greek citizens hostage with its riddle no one could answer: "What has four legs in the morning, two legs in the afternoon and three in the evening?"

New Kids on the Block are a terrible group sent as a plague by Maurice Starr, and hold radio listeners hostage with their riddle no one can answer: "How did five total white-bread dweebs get up the nerve to call their incredibly lame debut album *Hangin' Tough?"*

Orpheus reacted to the tragic death of his wife by descending into the dark and slime of the realm of the dead. He convinced the ghouls of the underworld that it was important that she be restored to life.

"Biographer" **Albert Goldman** reacted to the tragic death of John Lennon by descending into the dark and slime of celebrity exposés. He convinced the ghoulish public that it was important that false and vicious rumors about Lennon be brought to life.

DON MARTIN DEPT.

ONE TUESDAY MORNING

LETTER OPENERS DEPT.

WHAT'S IN A

DOW-JONES

IMPERIALISM

WOMEN'S LIBERATION MOVEMENT

WEIGHT WATCHERS

FOREIGN POLICY MAKERS

MID-EAST SITUATION

BRITAIN

WELFARE SYSTEM

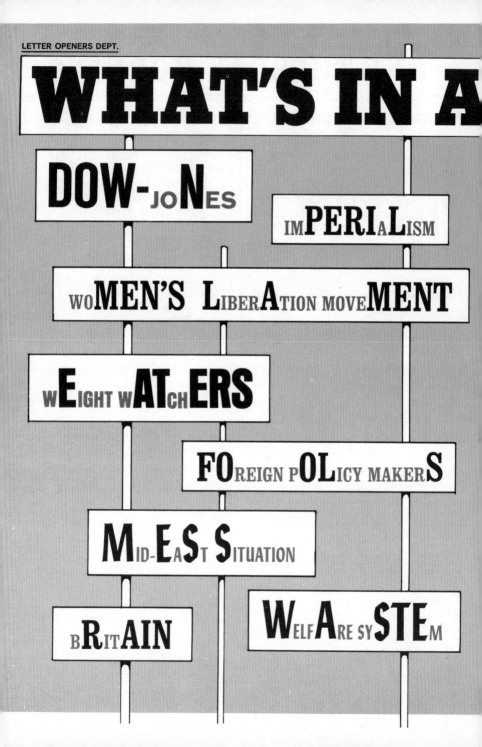

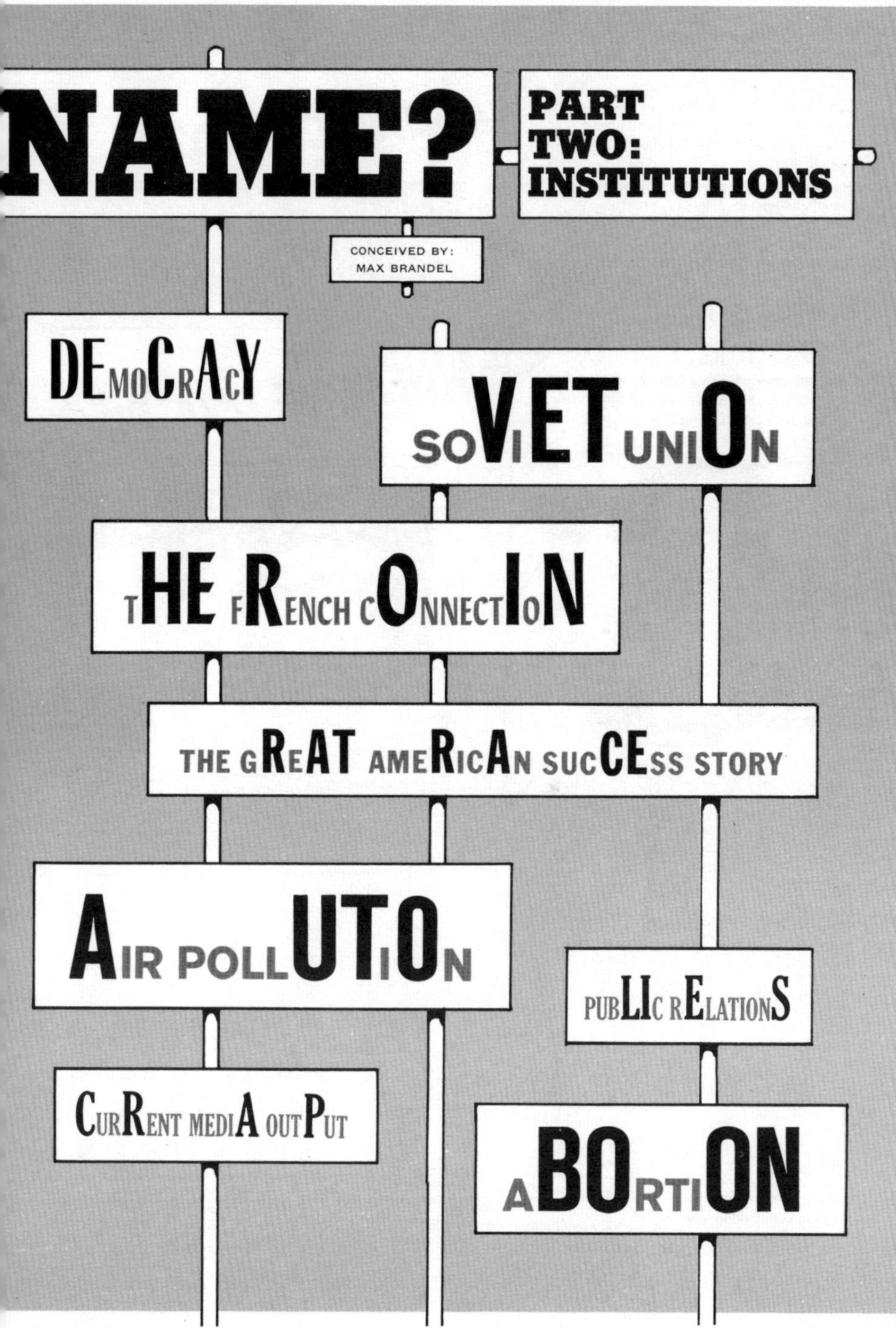
NAME?
PART TWO: INSTITUTIONS
CONCEIVED BY: MAX BRANDEL
DEMOCRACY
SOVIET UNION
THE FRENCH CONNECTION
THE GREAT AMERICAN SUCCESS STORY
AIR POLLUTION
PUBLIC RELATIONS
CURRENT MEDIA OUTPUT
ABORTION

LETTING THE GENE OUT OF THE BOTTLE DEPT.

In June of 2000, President Bill Clinton called a press conference to divert attention from yet another scandal...oh yeah, and also to announce the success of The Human Genome Project — a 7-year, multi-billion dollar effort by thousands of scientists to "map" our DNA for the first time in history. According to medical researchers, results from the Genome Project will enable us to cure diseases, prevent birth defects and slow the effects of aging. Yeah, yeah... big whoop. What WE found that was more interesting were these really...

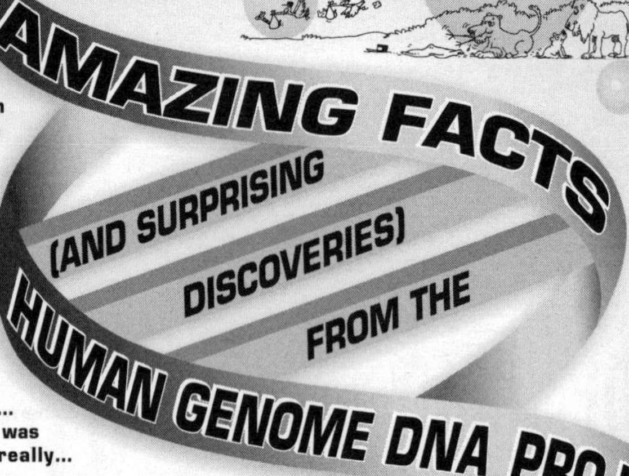

AMAZING FACTS (AND SURPRISING DISCOVERIES) FROM THE HUMAN GENOME DNA PROJECT

Homo sapiens share 99% of their genetic makeup with chimpanzees...but only 43% with the WWF's Chyna!

When a certain DNA string is played backwards on a gene-sequencing machine, it translates into "We can't believe you morons fell for that 'Paul is dead' gag we pulled back in '68! Signed, The Universe"!

Even with the success of the Human Genome Project, not a single American college student has been inspired to switch majors to Genetics from trendy, kick-back ones like Philosophy Of Women's Studies Through *Sex And The City* or Feng Shui For Your Minivan!

There is almost a 100% correlation between havi the gene for alcoholism and the gene for mistaken thinking the entire world wants to hear you sing Karaoke all friggin' night long!

ARTIST: PAUL COKER WRITER: MIKE SNIDER

entire Genome code of 3 billion C's, G's and T's is pronounced d, it sounds exactly like Gilbert Gottfried's standup act!

Incredibly, the genes for gullibility, judgementalism and joining the Republican Party are all right next to each other on the same chromosome!

The whole Human Genome can now be accessed on the Internet and, according to surveys, is more interesting than 57.8% of AOL chat rooms!

ong-accepted double-helix structure of DNA is ually only a single-helix; Watson & Crick were th drunk as hell from the lab Christmas party when they looked through the microscope!

The wealth of new scientific knowledge gained from the Genome Project virtually guarantees that, henceforth, every kid in America will flunk high school Biology the first time around and have to take it over again!

Congressmen and Senators are five times more likely to approve funding for Genetics research if the phrase "cloning Pamela Anderson" appears somewhere in the appropriations bill!

If the entire Human Genome were stretched out flat and laid end to end, it would be almost as long as the line of health insurers and drug companies looking to use that information to price-gouge and deny medical coverage!

MICROPHONIES DEPT.

THE MAD D

CHAPTER ONE

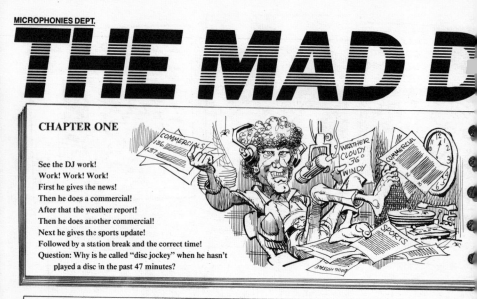

See the DJ work!
Work! Work! Work!
First he gives the news!
Then he does a commercial!
After that the weather report!
Then he does another commercial!
Next he gives the sports update!
Followed by a station break and the correct time!
Question: Why is he called "disc jockey" when he hasn't played a disc in the past 47 minutes?

CHAPTER THREE

Hear the studio technicians laughing!
Har! Har! Har!
They laugh at everything the DJ says!
"It's raining outside—lovely weather for ducks!"
Har! Har! Har!
Do they really think the DJ is funny and amusing?
Let's rephrase the question—Do they want to keep their jobs?
Har! Har! Har!

CHAPTER FIVE

Hear the DJ speckle his banter with interesting information!
Like how the gang at Via Veneto Ristorante on West 54th Street listen in every day!
And how Irma at A-1 Dry Cleaners on East 23rd Street wears the station's sweat shirt!
And how Vinnie, the expert mechanic at Sassone Auto Repair, personally requested this next great golden oldie!
What a nice guy the DJ is for passing out this valuable information!
Ever wonder where the DJ eats, has his clothes laundered, and his car fixed—for free?

. PRIMER

ARTIST:
JACK DAVIS

WRITER:
LOU SILVERSTONE

CHAPTER TWO

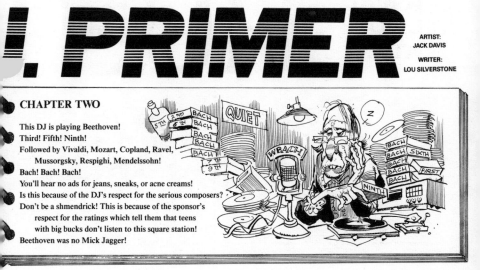

This DJ is playing Beethoven!
Third! Fifth! Ninth!
Followed by Vivaldi, Mozart, Copland, Ravel, Mussorgsky, Respighi, Mendelssohn!
Bach! Bach! Bach!
You'll hear no ads for jeans, sneaks, or acne creams!
Is this because of the DJ's respect for the serious composers?
Don't be a shmendrick! This is because of the sponsor's respect for the ratings which tell them that teens with big bucks don't listen to this square station!
Beethoven was no Mick Jagger!

CHAPTER FOUR

See the DJ is interviewing his guest!
He plays his guest's recordings!
He tells his guest how great he is!
At the show's end, he invites his guest to come back anytime!
Does he really like the guest that much?
Does he really think the guest is as wonderful as he said all show?
Don't be a shmendrick! The DJ likes anyone who'll do his show free!

CHAPTER SIX

See the angry man and lady!
They listen to this "zany" DJ every morning!
They listen to his vulgarity, obscenity, and blasts at the flag, mom, and apple pie!
Why do they listen to him?
So they can record all the vulgar and obscene things he says—and then write to the FCC demanding the DJ be taken off the air!

THE FOREST'S PRIME EVIL DEPT.

A MAD LOOK AT...

HUNT

ING

ARTIST & WRITER: SERGIO ARAGONES

MOOOOO!
RUMBLE!
BLAM!

1
BIRD GUIDE
BIRD WATCHERS
2
3
S.P.C.A
PROTECT OUR ENVIROMENT
DONT HUNT OUR
DON'T KILL OUR ANIMALS
SHH!
ARAGONES
FORD

ACOUSCHTICK DEPT.

In a recent issue, you may recall, we gave a timely and puckish lesson in onomatopoeias! We cleared up the popular misconception that an onomatopoeia is a Rumanian fish delicacy! In the likely event that you missed it, an onomatopoeia is a word that *sounds* like the thing it denotes—like "squish," for example. Anyway, we've continued our exhaustive research into this matter and we're exhausted. But as luck would have it, we've managed to milk another article out of this esoteric pap! We've discovered that if you listen carefully, you'll find that some noises actually sound like famous people's names. Confused? You won't be after checking out these...

CELEBRIT

Y SOUND EFFECTS

ARTIST AND WRITER: JOHN CALDWELL

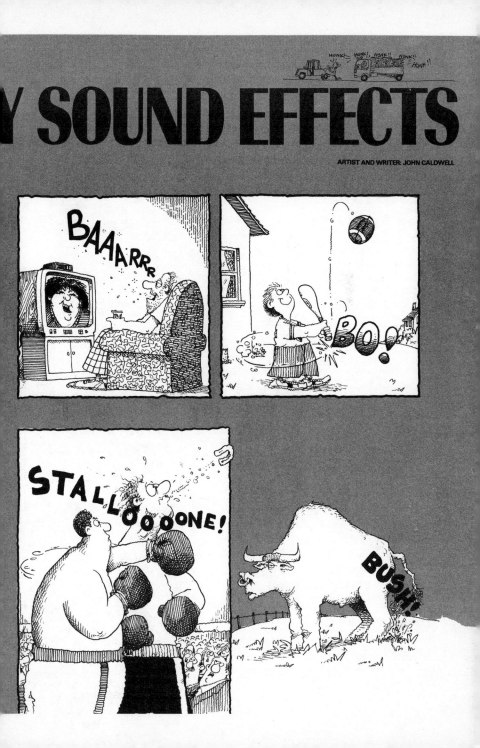

AN EMBARRASSMENT OF RICHARD'S DEPT.

Did you ever notice that a three-step ladder has a big label on it warning you not to use the top two steps? And that light fixture instructions tell you what wattage to use "to reduce risk of fire"? Why all this over-cautiousness?

WARNING LABELS

Designed to Head Off

ARTIST: BOB CLARKE WRITER: DICK DEBARTOLO

ROAD CHIEF SUPER BIKE

WARNING: Do not ride this bicycle on highways, streets, roads, sidewalks or any other surfaces not recommended by manufacturer.

Protective gloves, footgear, helmet, goggles and body padding **must be worn** by rider as well as anyone standing in the vicinity of this bicycle.

Attempting to balance yourself on two wheels can result in **physical injury.**

Manufacturer **assumes no responsibility** for consequences if bicycle is ridden at speeds in excess of one (1) mile per hour.

STICKY STUFF GLUE®

DO NOT use Sticky Stuff Glue® on Plastic, Wood, Paper, Fabric or any other materials not expressly covered by our warranty.

Once tube is open, DO NOT inhale or exhale within a two-mile radius of this product.

Store unused portion at Room Temperature, but UNDER NO CIRCUMSTANCE should it be stored indoors.

Any and all leftover glue MUST BE DISPOSED OF using Federally Approved Guidelines for explosives and other hazardous toxic materials.

HI-GENE—*the sanitary straw*

SAFETY GUIDELINES

1. Removal of paper wrapper will result in contamination of straw due to atmospheric bacteria, voiding any and all sanitary claims made by manufacturer.
2. Placement of straw in hot, cold or warm liquids will severely shorten the life expectancy of this product.
3. Do not place either end of straw in mouth or gagging may occur.
4. For maximum protection against germs and possible infection, manufacturer recommends discarding straw after each sip and using a new one.

Simple! In an attempt to limit their liability from lawsuits, manufacturers are putting more and more warnings on their products. How far will this warning trend go? Probably to new heights of stupidity! You'll see as we now look at...

OF THE FUTURE Potential Lawsuits

WARNING: The purchaser of this magazine assumes all responsibility for any loss of braincells that may result from reading this article.

SNOWMAN Air Conditioner

FOR SAFE OPERATION OF YOUR SNOWMAN AIR CONDITIONER, FOLLOW THESE SAFETY RULES CAREFULLY!

a. Shut off main power source to your entire block before plugging unit into a properly-wired electrical outlet.

b. Do not place this unit on a window sill without first supporting sill with cast iron I-beams.

c. Under no circumstance should this unit be used in areas of high humidity or extreme heat.

d. Touching or adjusting knobs while unit is running is not recommended. To adjust Temperature Setting from low to medium or medium to high cool, shut off unit, adjust setting and wait six hours before restarting.

HAMMER

READ BEFORE USING

DO NOT use your Big Hit Hammer to strike any object other than household nails appearing on our approved list of authorized household nails.

BE SURE to allow hammer to cool off between strikes.

FOR SAFEST RESULTS, use your Big Hit hammer only under the strict supervision of a Professionally Licensed Carpenter.

LITTLE INDIAN TOY BOW & ARROW SET

WARNING! THIS TOY IS NOT A TOY! **WARNING!**

- **Do not view or open this package unless in the presence of an adult American Indian.**
- **Keep arrows in a secure place, far away from bow.**
- **Keep bow in a secure place, far away from arrows.**
- **Under no circumstance should this bow be used to shoot arrows at any person, animal, object or target!**

SHOP THERAPY DEPT.

DUCK EDWING HANGS THE

ARTIST AND

OUT AT
MALL

CK EDWING

STOP! THIEF!

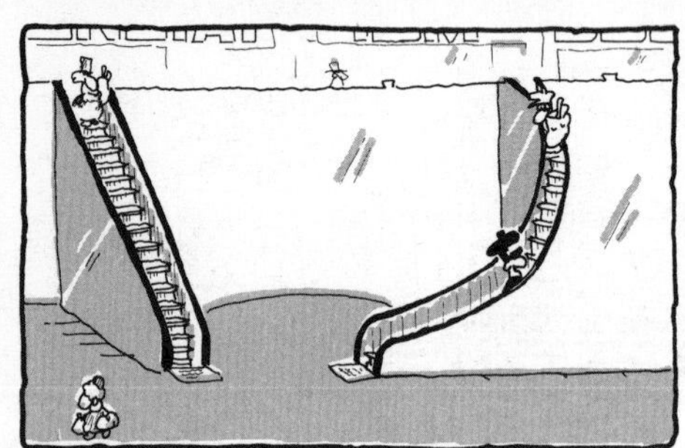

TROMP! TROMP!

STOP! THIEF!
TROMP! TROMP!

TROMP! TROMP!

DID YOU CATCH HIM?
ARE YOU KIDDING?!? HE HAD AT LEAST A NINE-STEP LEAD ON THE ESCALATOR!

ZODIACS MURDER DEPT.

YOUR MAD HOROSCOPE

TODAY'S BIRTHDAY:

Loved ones are grateful if you try not to spit while blowing out the candles on your cake.

ARIES
March 21—April 19

A strange shifting in the stars may cause you to experience some pleasure while viewing a rerun of Sheriff Lobo. Do not worry. This is only an illusion, and will pass, like a cheap meal. Do not treat lovemaking as a hobby or you could do permanent damage to yourself with wrongful applications of model airplane glue.

TAURUS
April 20—May 20

Your enthusiasm is contagious and so is your rash, so lay off the romantic entanglements. Complete one project before begining a second. However, it is not necessary to complete one project if you're planning to move directly on to a third. Your grades can improve overnight, providing you write legibly on your arm.

GEMINI
May 21—June 21

After years of diligent brown-nosing, you rise to the upper echelons of corporate power. Too bad your company is about to go under! This is typical of the way your luck has been running recently and will continue to run for some time. Do not fret! You still have a lot of drive left in you. Take a trip to Detroit!

MOON CHILDREN
June 22—July 22

The position of your stars is identical to those of Aquarius, Capricorn and Sagittarius. How this can be, we don't know. (But it does go a long way in explaining your lack of originality in life!) We suggest that from now on you read those three horoscopes and then pick out any advice you think looks good to you.

LEO
July 23—August 22

Your main stars have shifted in such a way that, when connected by straight lines, they strongly resemble either a profile of Alexander Haig or an aerial view of New Jersey. (This is open to artistic interpretation.) Such a configuration strongly suggests that you will soon be overtaken by a desire to invade Secaucus.

VIRGO
August 23—September 22

Give a hand at home. Get ahead at work. Give a passing stranger the eye, and a passing motorist the finger. Lose an arm and a leg at the track. Get something off your chest. Lend your ears to fellow countrymen. Stick your nose in other people's business. Get your ass in a sling. Put your foot in your mouth. Hang loose.

LIBRA
September 23—October 23

The position of Yank, the main star influencing your destiny, advises that now is an excellent time for a torrid romantic fling. However, the position of the Moral Majority condemns a torrid romantic fling as a no-no. The choice is yours. Either be bored out of your skull on earth, or burn for all eternity in hell!

SCORPIO
October 24—November 21

A good day! An annoying neighbor will cease to bother you as you are evicted in the AM. Improve your personal ties by throwing out the very wide ones with the polka dot prints. Nobody has been wearing them for years! Look for your mailbox to be flooded with letters as someone pours an entire can of alphabet soup in it.

SAGITTARIUS
November 22—December 21

A study of your stars has failed to uncover any information about your future. This could mean that you have no future. In fact, it's quite possible that you recently passed away, and your loved ones have been derelict in making the proper arrangements. Seek the advice of an expert, however, before having yourself cremated.

CAPRICORN
December 22—January 19

Take a chance on a new co-worker. They're only a dollar each and, who knows, you may just win her! The AM may seem horrible today, however, it will begin to look better and better once you see what the PM has in store for you. An unexpected raise and promotion at work enables you to pay for your emergency brain surgery.

AQUARIUS
January 20—February 18

Your Moon has very quietly moved from the House of Leo to the Condominium of Stanley. (Tax Purposes.) This signals a dramatic upheaval in your emotional state. Warm thoughts will singe your brain. Because Uranus and your piles are one, you could be in big danger! Beware of fools, envious of your many shortcomings.

PISCES
February 19—March 20

A sensational day! An unexpected romance blooms out of a chance encounter at a local vigilante meeting. Be frank with your boss. That way, when you screw up, he will fire Frank and not you! Put your priorities in alphabetical order and stop accepting second best. It's much too good for you!

WRITER: JOHN FICARRA

RED-HOT PEPPER-FLAVORED TONGUE DEPRESSORS

No need to describe the hysterical reaction when you use one of these on your patients!

PORNOGRAPHIC INK BLOTS

Dirty pictures cleverly hidden in Rorschach cards! Ask them what they see... and they'll be too ashamed to tell you! Lots of laughs!!

ITCHING PLASTER CASTS

Mix our "Itching Powder" into the plaster before applying any type cast! Drives 'em crazy!

TRYING YOUR PATIENTS DEPT.

Attention, all you Doctors out there! It's time you exploded once and for all the myth that Doctors are serious people, intent on healing the sick, with no

MAD'S PRAC CATALOGUE F

ARTIST: AL JAFFEE

COWS' INTESTINES

Leave these lying around Post-Op, and watch their faces when they come to!

FUNNY INSTRUMENT BAG

Contains 8" needles, rusty saws, bent pliers, One look and they pass out!

BLURRY EYE CHARTS

Watch them squint, strain and rub their eyes while you howl with laughter!

me for foolishness and no sense of humor. (By the way, what are you doing, ading MAD?!) You can accomplish this impossible task by using the items in

TICAL JOKE OR DOCTORS

RITER: BEPPE SABATINI

MANGLED I.D. BRACELETS

ip one of these into a patient's plate of hash before the Orderly takes his tray of hospital food. Yeow! Perfect for your stubborn overweights!

"PLEASE DISROBE" SIGNS

scream! Put them in your waiting room, your hallway, your lobby—every-here! Then, switch 'em all on! Your office'll look like a Nudist Colony!

RUBBER NOSES

p one of these onto your nose job patient before she comes out of the esthetic! When she does, she'll take one look and go through the roof!

FAKE PRESCRIPTIONS

Each one has pre-printed swear words in Latin! Watch 'em get punched out by their Pharmacist!

ADULT-PROOF PILL BOTTLES

Watch as they struggle for hours because these special bottles cannot be opened! Perfect for hypochondriac (and other complaining) patients!

DRIBBLING SPECIMEN BOTTLES

Wait'll they try carrying these into your Lab!

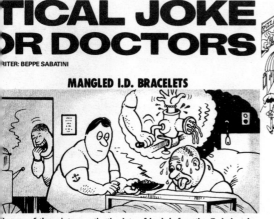

FRANK ON A ROLL DEPT.

We've all sung about Old MacDonald and his cows and pigs and sheep. But farming has changed, and these days he's got more to contend with than the old "moo-moo here" and "oink-oink there." As you'll see in this updated version of...

OLD Ma

Old MacDonald farmed the land—E-I-E-I-O!
But failed to prosper as he'd planned—E-I-E-I-O!
With a wheat blight here and a corn blight there—
Here a blight, there a blight, ev'ry crop a sad sight;
Old MacDonald lost four grand—E-I-E-I-O!

Old MacDonald, smart guy he—E-I-E-I-O!
Sprayed all his crops with DDT—E-I-E-I-O!
With a cough, cough here and a hack, hack there—
Here a choke, there a choke, worse than cig-a-rette smoke;
A wheat blight here and a corn blight there—
Here a blight, there a blight, ev'ry crop a sad sight;
Old MacDonald groaned "Why me?"—E-I-E-I-O!

Old MacDonald prayed for rain—E-I-E-I-O!
To save his rotting fields of grain—E-I-E-I-O!
With a dry spell here and a dry spell there—
Here a drought, there a drought, ev'ry harvest wiped out;
A cough, cough here and a hack, hack there—
Here a choke, there a choke, worse than cig-a-rette smoke;
A wheat blight here and a corn blight there—
Here a blight, there a blight, ev'ry crop a sad sight;
Old MacDonald prayed in vain—E-I-E-I-O!

DONALD

ARTIST: GERRY GERSTEN

IDEA: DAN LOZER WRITER: FRANK JACOBS

Old MacDonald, sad to say—E-I-E-I-O!
Had cred-i-tors he could not pay—E-I-E-I-O!
With a seed bill here, a manure bill there—
Here a debt, there a debt, making ulcers worse yet;
A dry spell here and a dry spell there—
Here a drought, there a drought, ev'ry harvest wiped out;
A cough, cough here and a hack, hack there—
Here a choke, there a choke, worse than cig-a-rette smoke;
A wheat blight here and a corn blight there—
Here a blight, there a blight, ev'ry crop a sad sight;
Old MacDonald moaned "Oy vey!"—E-I-E-I-O!

Old MacDonald, sought relief—E-I-E-I-O!
He called D.C. and hailed the chief—E-I-E-I-O!
Got a con job here and a snow job there—
Here a stall, there a stall, up against a stone wall;
A seed bill here, a manure bill there—
Here a debt, there a debt, making ulcers worse yet;
A dry spell here and a dry spell there—
Here a drought, there a drought, ev'ry harvest wiped out;
A cough, cough here and a hack, hack there—
Here a choke, there a choke, worse than cig-a-rette smoke;
A wheat blight here and a corn blight there—
Here a blight, there a blight, ev'ry crop a sad sight;
Old MacDonald cried "Good Grief!"—E-I-E-I-O!

Old MacDonald got bad news—E-I-E-I-O!
His bank refused his IOUs—E-I-E-I-O!
With a "Screw you!" here and a "Screw you!" there—
Land they took, cows they took, wiping out the poor schnook;
Got a con job here, and snow job there—
Here a stall, there a stall, up against a stone wall;
A seed bill here, a manure bill there—
Here a debt, there a debt, making ulcers worse yet;
A dry spell here and a dry spell there—
Here a drought, there a drought, ev'ry harvest wiped out;
A cough, cough here and a hack, hack there—
Here a choke, there a choke, worse than cig-a-rette smoke;
A wheat blight here and a corn blight there—
Here a blight, there a blight, ev'ry crop a sad sight;
OLD MacDONALD NOW SELLS SHOES—E-I-E-I-O!

ONE DAY ON THE HIGHWAY

FRANK ON A ROLL DEPT.

It's another Election Year. Once again incumbent and upstart politicians are crawling out from the sewers and vying for various political offices around the country. Because there are so many candidates, the Primary System was devised as a way of winnowing the field... separating the wheat from the chaff...allowing the cream to rise to the top. This process used to work! But no more! You'll see what we mean as you rhyme along with the following...

10 LITTLE CANDIDATES

Ten little candidates,
Their records in review;
One took some "contributions"
From an S&L or two;
Said he, "Somebody set me up;
The charges I deny;"
This brings our number down to nine;
Oh, sure, and horses fly.

ARTIST: PAUL COKER WRITER: FRANK JACOBS

Ten little candidates,
Still in the race somehow;
There's one, we hear, who dodged the draft;
Said he, "Don't have a cow!"
I sweated bullets building my
Political career;"
You'd think by now there would be eight;
Get real! They're all still here.

Ten little candidates,
All upright gents, you'd think;
One bounced a hundred checks or so,
Which caused an awful stink;
Said he, "I've been the victim of
An underhanded plot;"
In case you wonder where we stand,
We're down to seven—NOT!

Ten little candidates,
All claiming that they care;
One lobbied for a logging firm
That stripped a forest bare;
He's got an offshore drilling plan
That scares us half to death;
We should be down to six by now;
Oh, yeah? Don't hold your breath.

Ten little candidates,
Still running, if you please;
Said one, "To save our country,
We must crush the Japanese!
The imports that they dump on us,"
He said, "must soon be gone,"
Then drove off in his Subaru;
We're down to five? Dream on!

Ten little candidates,
All getting in their licks;
One smeared his foe with TV ads,
Midst other dirty tricks;
Said he, "My staffers are to blame;
They planned it all themselves;"
Which brings our number down to four
If you believe in elves.

Ten little candidates,
Each hoping to prevail;
One came out with a budget plan
That's guaranteed to fail;
If he gets in, our lives will be
More screwed up than they are;
You say we should be down to three?
Nice try, but no cigar.

Ten little candidates,
Each pondering his fate;
One claimed he was "pro-family"
While cheating on his mate;
Said he, "Don't take some bimbo's word—
She's only spouting lies;"
Guess what? The number hasn't changed;
Surprise! Surprise! Surprise!

Ten little candidates,
Still with the urge to run;
One tickled crowds with racial jokes;
Said he, "'Twas all in fun;
The darkies know I'm on their side;
I've got one on my staff;"
What's that? You think we're down to one?
Ha-ha! It is to laugh.

Ten little candidates,
Who will not disappear,
And please don't ask us to explain
How come they're all still here;
We'll find out on Election Day
Which one the voters choose,
Although, by now, it should be clear
Whoever wins, we lose.

FIGHTING

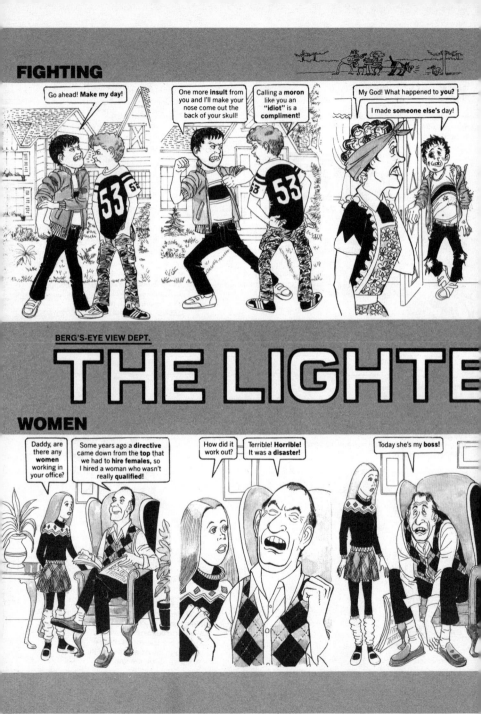

BERG'S-EYE VIEW DEPT.

THE LIGHTE

WOMEN

FINANCES

R SIDE OF...

ARTIST & WRITER:
DAVE BERG

WEDDINGS

JOGGING

CRIME

COMMUNICATION

TELEVISION

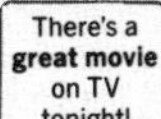

COMPANY

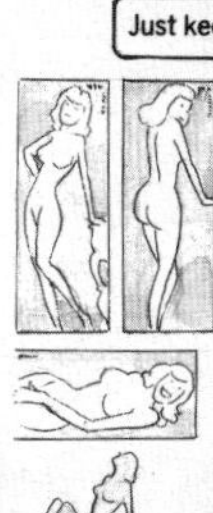

HEALTH

RELATIONSHIPS

SCHOOL

ADJUSTING THE VOLUMES DEPT.

Many of us are familiar with the titles of famous books of the past—even if we never bothered to actually take the time to read any of them! Their authors gave them the titles they thought were most appropriate at the time. But if those same books were written today, their names would probably be somewhat different to reflect our modern times. To see what we mean, check out...

MAD'S UPDATED BOOK TITLES

FOR THE 90'S

MS. MINIVER

ARTIST: BOB CLARKE WRITER: WILLIAM GARVIN

ATTENTION K. MARX SHOPPERS DEPT.

EVERYTHING MUST GO!

With the recent stunning collapse of many Communist regimes all over the world, it may just be a matter of time until we see ads for the...

WORLD COM

Dros Vyutnya! I'm CRAZY GORBY, here with loads of used Glasnost bargains! Just look at our first item: **25,000 Plaster Busts of Lenin!** They can easily be converted into busts of your favorite Western heroes, including Shakespeare, Frank Zappa, Steven Spielberg and more!

ARTIST: JOHN POU

You'll want several of these ... The **Official Jockstrap of the Soviet "Women's" Olympic Weight Lifting Team!** The 1984 Olympics boycott left us with too many, but our loss is your gain!

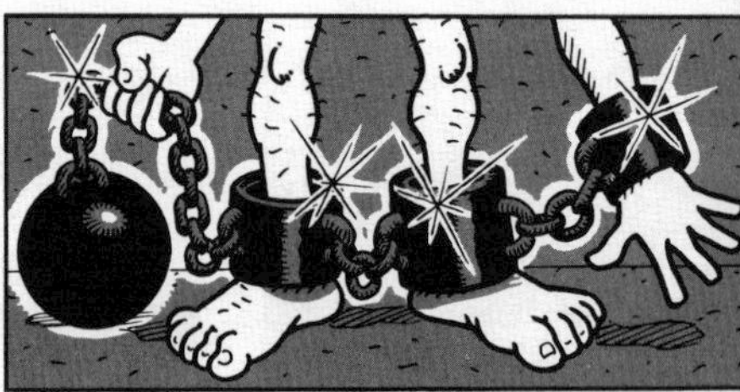

Here we have some lovely **Wrist and Ankle "Jewelry" from Siberia!** They were formerly used to restrain inmates ... uh, mental patients, who were all miraculously "cured" when I took over the government!

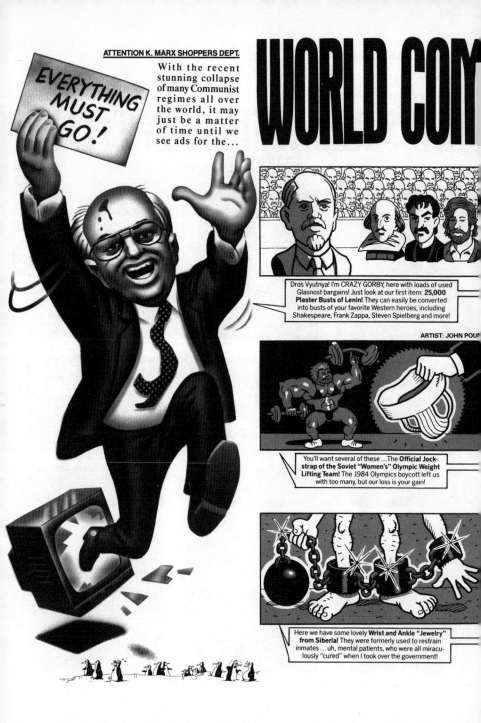

MUNISM CLOSE-OUT SALE

Need paper to jot down phone messages and shopping lists? Try these **Pre-Marked Ballot Note Pads!** Before Glasnost, we printed up a 10-year supply of already-filled-out voter ballots! Luckily, they're as one-sided as the elections we planned to use them for!

We've got boxcars full of **Marxist-Version History Books**... Every one a comedy classic! Just listen to these titles: "Stalin: Prince of Peace," "1979: The Soviet Rescue of Afghanistan," "The Happy Days of Mao's Cultural Revolution" and hundreds more!

WRITER: MIKE SNIDER

We've recently removed all of our **Electronic Bugs** from the American Embassy in Moscow and they can be yours! Each listening device is KGB-guaranteed for one full year!

Men! Check out these **Custom Soviet Ill-Fitting Suits!** We've got racks and racks of 'em! For proper fit, be sure to specify a size OTHER than your own!

Here's a handyman's special: **127,345,000 Gallons of Drab Socialist Paint!** Available in gray, off-gray, brownish-gray and other depressing grays!

Hoo-boy! pick up a few of our **10,000 East German Border Dogs** and never fear intruders in your home again! These easy-to-care-for pups eat anything—or anyone!

Hey, Comrades! Forget the Berlin Wall! Give the souvenir that GLOWS in the DARK! **A Piece of Chernobyl!**

And look at this great **free T-shirt** you'll get with every $25 purchase! Order now! I don't know how much longer they—or I—will last!

GOODNIGHT KISS-OFF DEPT.

HOW TO END PAINLE

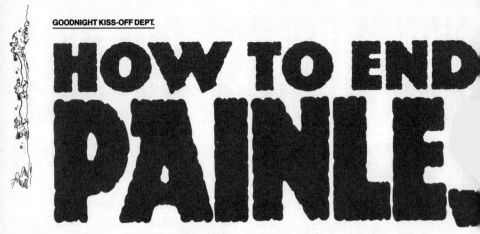

I know holds that can paralyze a 200 pound linebacker!

Have you ever been to a baby lamb slaughter house? It's brutal!

I gotta get outta here! There's my truant officer and I'm supposed to be in my social studies class now!

Let's walk past the Post Office, I'd like to see if my picture is still hanging!
PORGES

A DATE
SLY

Oops! Nine-thirty! Time to call my parole officer!

ARTIST AND WRITER: PAUL PETER PORGES

It's a mysterious rash that has medical science baffled!

Why pay top dollar for tickets when we stand a good chance of sneaking into this concert free!

I ordered live snails for two!

Can you cash my unemployment check?

What's in a movie title? Maybe a hidden, true review! Here's . . .

MAD'S INSTANT MOVIE

IT'S THE REEL ZING DEPT.
REVIEWS
QUIGLEY DOWN UNDER
FLIGHT OF THE INTRUDER
STAR TREK V: THE FINAL FRONTIER
DICK TRACY
BONFIRE OF THE VANITIES
ANOTHER 48 HOURS
GREMLINS 2: THE NEW BATCH
ACK TO THE FUTURE PART III
THE FABULOUS BAKER BOYS

DON MARTIN DEPT.

LATE ONE NIGHT IN A WATERFRONT TAVERN

MAKING A MESSAGE OF THINGS DEPT.

For years, motorists have been driving by road signs and reading them one at a time, even though it's far more telling to read them as a group! Yes, their true meanings are easily seen when...

When Roadside Signs Overlap

ARTIST: GEORGE WOODBRIDGE WRITER: HENRY CLARK

Jack LaLanne
European & Holiday Spas
BOY
OH
BOY
I
ache
all
OVER
Bob's BIG BOY
Audi
LAWN-BOY SNAPPER
Prudential Bache
Rexall DRUGS & STUFF
RANGE ROVER
Can
Carve
up
Bank
ROLLS
At
BLOCKBUSTER
Speedy
WELCOME TO Atlantic City STRAIGHT AHEAD
Canon AUTHORIZED DEALER
Carvel
United Parcel Service
BankLeumi BRANCH OFFICE
ROLLS ROYCE
Atlas Van Lines
VIDEO RENTALS
Speedy muffler king
BRENNER BY-PASS 2 MILES
WIN 1
For
SUB
STANDARD
Travel
GO GREYHOUND
AND LEAVE THE DRIVING TO US
Wm RIGBY & SON AUTHORIZED SERVICE CENTER
Ray Devoe's SUBARU
27 MILES
The Travelers
BOSTON TO AUSTIN
GREYHOUND
412

MAY
BE
Prudent
TO
ARM
ENTERING
Philadelphia
CITY OF BROTHERLY LOVE
MAYTAG
BEKINS
VAN LINES
LOCAL OFFICE
Prudential
INSURANCE
TORO
TORO POWER MOWER
ARMSTRONG
TIRES
VISIT
NATIONAL
ENQUIRER
LARGEST CIRCULATION OF ANY PAPER IN AMERICA
A
N
ATIONWIDE
hack
PRESS
YAMAHA
NATIONWIDE
INSURANCE
Radio Shack
FEDERAL EXPRESS
DROP-OFF
Party Time EXPRESS
NEW PRESIDENT OF HARVARD
Be
Stuck
ON
A
BRIDGE
All
DAY
VISIT
NEW YORK
CITY
HON.
DAVY RINKYDINKY
MAYOR & CHIEF POOBAH
I♥NY TOURISM COMMISSION
Bendix
Stuckey's
RESTAURANTS
ONKYO
AMOCO
BRIDGESTONE
SERVICE SALES
Allstate
You're in good hands.
DAYS INN
MIGHTY MAX KORN'S
TARHEEL TOURS
DWEEB

A
Good
STATE
TO
be
Old
IN
ENTERING
Florida
Alamo Rent A Car
Good Humor
STATE FARM
Auto Life Fire
INSURANCE
TOSHIBA
benetton
LIND Oldsmobile
INTERNATIONAL
TRUCKS
J. ALTZ HEIMER TRANS.
SENIOR CITIZEN VAN
SENIOR CITIZEN TRANSPORT
FAST, SAFE TRANSPORT
Cooke RETIREMENT
ZZZZZ
27
INVALID COACH
Sunshine
Get
Pan
Fried
GOO
AT
Pizza Hut
Getty SERVICE
Panasonic BOOM BOXES
Friedrich
AUTHORIZED SERVICE CENTER
GOODYEAR
TIRES DEALER TIRES
AT&T
ROAD BUSTER
CAUTION
DEAR XING
DUMP BUSH VOTE DEMOCRATIC IN '92
HE
LIED
TO
US
OVER
TAX
e's
PORSCHE
SALES SERVICE
ALLIED VAN LINES
1HOUR PHOTO
LEXUS
HOOVER
PENTAX SALES • SERVICE
Hardee's RESTAURANTS
BOOK OF VIABLE IDEAS FOR '92
RDMYLPS1
U.S.
GW

JOKE AND DAGGER DEPT.

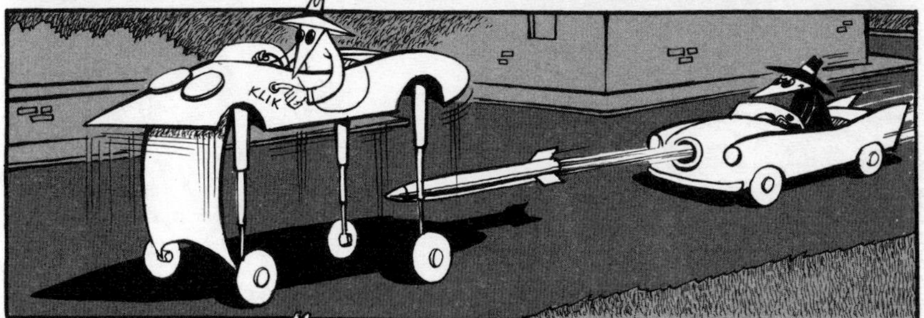

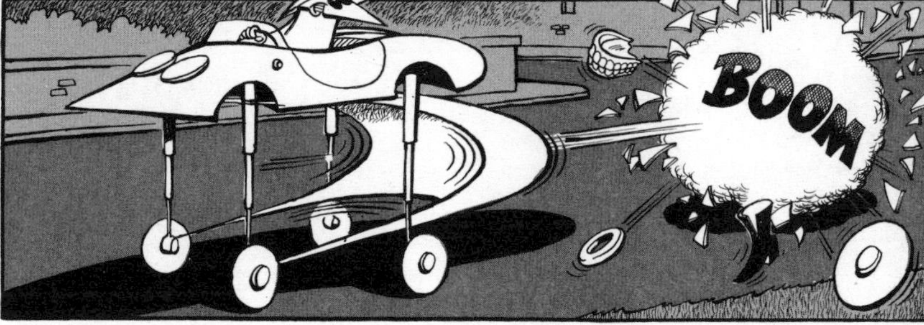

TEACHING THEM A LISTEN DEPT.

Don't you wish there was some way of gettin[g] even with the obnoxious creeps who listen i[n] on private conversations? Then rejoice! Ther[e]

EAVESD
SHOO

ARTIST: BOB JON

AT THE OFFICE

AT A RESTAURANT

AT A DOCTOR'S OFFICE

s!! The next time your personal chatter is uned-in to by unwanted ears, give 'em more han they bargained for with MAD's patented…

ROPPER-
KERS

VRITER: MIKE SNIDER

IN A CLASSROOM

IN ADJOINING APARTMENTS

ON AN AIRPLANE

PHASING REALITY DEPT.

It is widely believed that a person experiences four psychological phases when grieving over death. They are: Denial—you refuse to believe the obvious; Anger—you get really pissed off at the circumstances; Depression—you become distressed at the realization; Acceptance—okay, you just deal with it. Here at MAD, we figured that there are some other situations in life when people experience these same grieving phases! So, we will now ask you to look at yourself and your emotions as you read up on...

BEING FAT

DENIAL

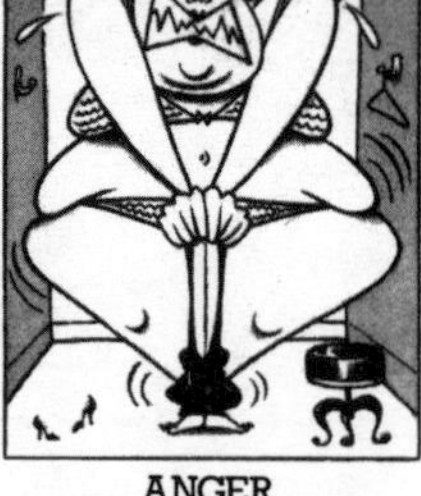

ANGER

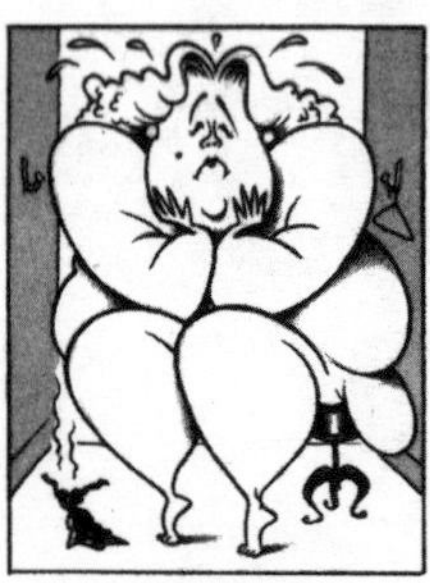

DEPRESSION

ACCEPTANCE

AGING

DENIAL

ANGER

DEPRESSION

ACCEPTANCE

BEING LOST

DENIAL

ANGER

DEPRESSION

ACCEPTANCE

MAD STAGES OF...

ARTIST AND WRITER: RICK TULKA

BALDNESS

DENIAL

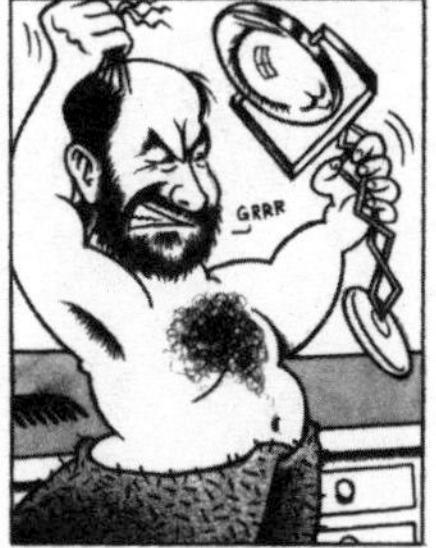

ANGER

DEPRESSION

ACCEPTANCE

NAUSEA

DENIAL

ANGER

DEPRESSION

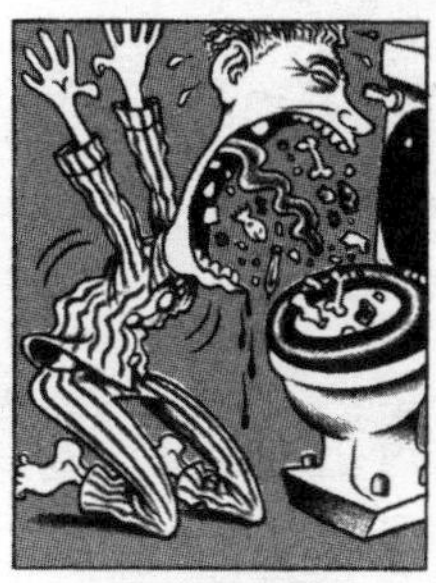

ACCEPTANCE

STUPIDITY

DENIAL

ANGER

DEPRESSION

ACCEPTANCE

BEAU JEST DEPT.

It's said "True love is a many splendor thing," and this being the case, every girl longs to me her perfect match, her own Prince Charming, the proverbial Mr. "Right." Unfortunately, it's als said, "A good man is hard to find" and this makes finding Mr. "Right" more difficult than findin

GUYS YOU'RE LIKELY TO MEET BEFC

ARTIST: ALYSE NEWMA

MR. "RIGHT—'TIL YOU MENTION THE WORD 'MARRIAGE'"

MR. "RIGHT OUT OF THE 60'S"

MR. "RIGHT INTO THE BACK SEAT"

MR. "RIGHT AWAY, MOTHER!"

MR. "RIGHT AFTER THE POST-GAME SHOW"

MR. "RIGHT OFF THE ASSEMBLY LINE"

an intelligent person in the audience of the Morton Downey, Jr. Show! We don't mean to discourage you ladies, but the sad truth is you'll probably get involved with an impressive bunch of losers before you finally find the fellow for you. So brace yourself for the worst, 'cause here are the...

RE MR. 'RIGHT'

WRITER: MIKE SNIDER

MR. "RIGHT GUARD CANDIDATE"

MR. "RIGHT ON, OLLIE NORTH!"

MR. "RIGHT DOWN THE MIDDLE"

MR. "RIGHT INTO INTENSIVE CARE GO YOUR PARENTS!"

MR. "RIGHT AFTER MY DIVORCE, BABE"

MR. "RIGHTSIDE-DOWN"

WISE GUIDES DEPT.

Remember the time you played Red Rover with your friends and you got ready to run and break through their locked arms? Remember your surprise when instead your so-called "friends" held

RULES FOR GAMES THE WA

BATTLESHIP (for 2-year-olds)

1. Steal game from underneath your brother's bed.

2. Swallow all of the little plastic ships.

3. Go to the hospital to have your stomach pumped.

4. Add up points for each ship the doctor recovers from your stomach.

5. If you get 10 or more points, you win!

ARTIST: JACK DAVIS

SCRABBLE (for 8 to 14-year-olds)

1. Make sure that all parents and adults are a safe distance away from the board.

2. Each player grabs a handful of letters.

3. All players take turns trying to spell the most obscene, profane and foul words they can think of.

4. Award extra points for dirty words with more than four letters and for medical terms.

you down and ran off with your shorts? You fool! Games NEVER stick to regulation play! To prepare you for those unexpected developments (sorry, we can't retrieve your shorts), MAD presents...

Y THEY'RE REALLY PLAYED

TRIVIAL PURSUIT (for 60-year-olds)

1. Play the game normally until a question comes up about MTV, Nintendo, or Madonna.

2. Stop the game and start talking about the good old days before there was any such thing as MTV, Nintendo or Madonna.

3. Eat a big bowl of fiber and go to bed early.

VRITER: MICHAEL GOODWIN

FOOTBALL (for 7 to 10-year-olds)

1. Begin playing in a friendly manner.

2. Continue until one team outscores the other by 50 points.

3. If you are the losing team, begin to play dirty.

4. When a fight breaks out, erase the score.

5. The team with the least amount of players to run home crying wins!

DODGEBALL (for 8 to 13-year-olds)

1. Have all the popular kids form a circle around all the unpopular kids.

2. Peg all the girls first to get them out of the way.

3. Use the inflatable rubber ball until there is only one boy left in the middle.

4. If he is too fast to be hit with the ball, see if he can dodge sticks and rocks.

5. When the boy quits, or is knocked unconscious, everyone in the circle wins!

HIDE AND SEEK (for 40-year-olds playing with 3-year-olds)

1. Explain the rules to your annoying, hyperactive 3-year-old nephew.

2. Tell him to go hide and not come out till you find him.

3. Go sit in your favorite easy chair and enjoy the silence.

4. Occasionally yell out, "I'm going to get you!" so the little brat stays hidden.

5. Continue using these rules until his mother finally comes to pick him up.

DON MARTIN DEPT.

ONE NIGHT IN A POLICE STATION

SERGIO ARAGONES DEPT.

A MAD LOOK AT FAST F

ARTIST AND WRITER

OOD

ERGIO ARAGONES

THE OL' CELL GAME DEPT.

Today's streets are filled with people carrying radios, TVs, calculators, and computers. Soon they will also be filled with something else—Dead Batteries! With that in mind, here's

NEW USES

Chess Pieces

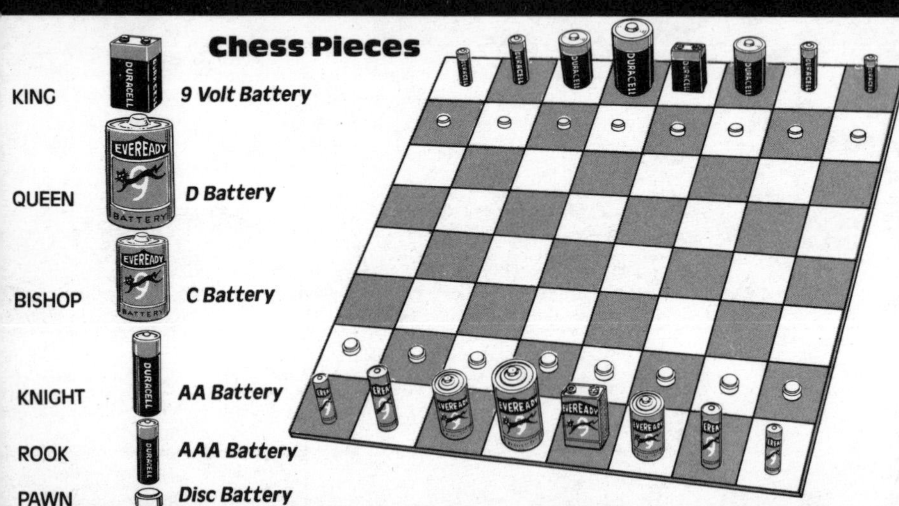

ARTIST & WRITER: AL JAFFEE

Ear Plugs

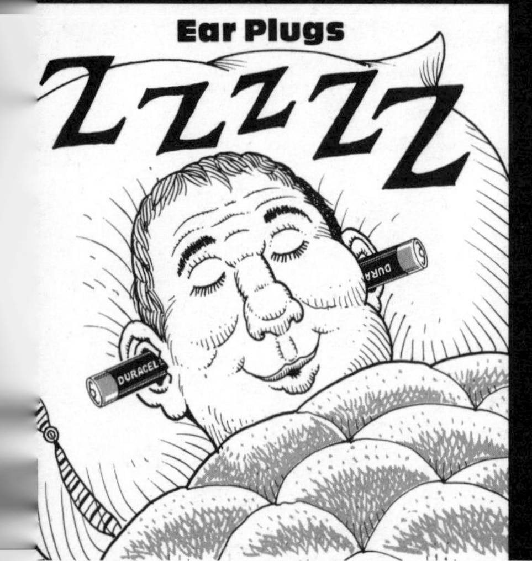

Cuckoo Clock Weights

FOR OLD BATTERIES

Hair Curlers

Scale Weights

Executive Desk Toy

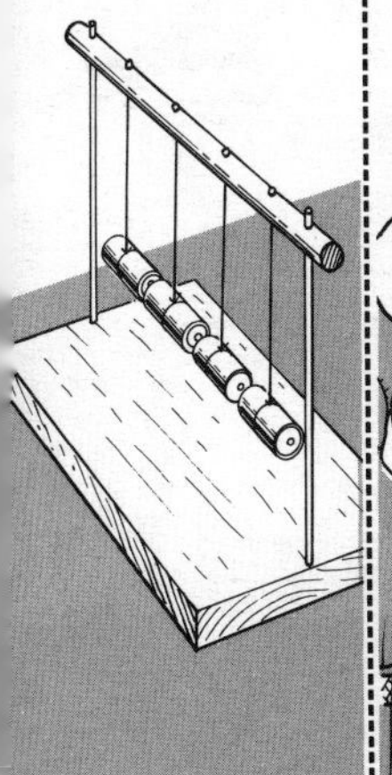

PREDICTABILITY

BERG'S-EYE VIEW DEPT.

THE LIGHTE

SPEEDING

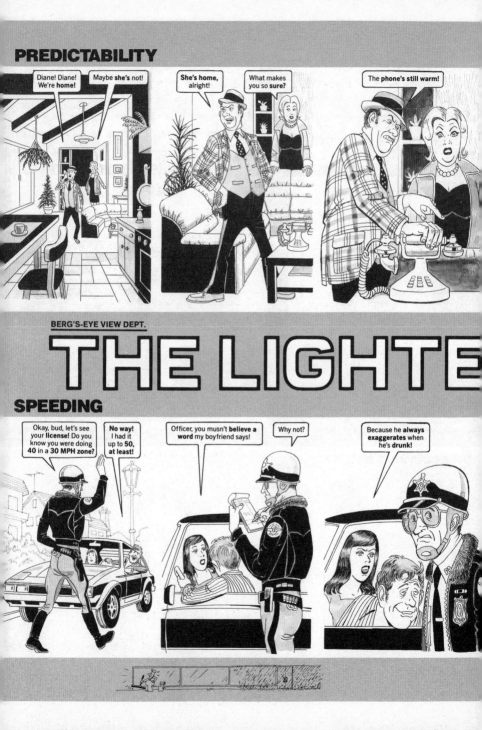

ADDICTION

R SIDE OF...

ARTIST & WRITER: DAVE BERG

WEDDINGS

COMMUNICATION

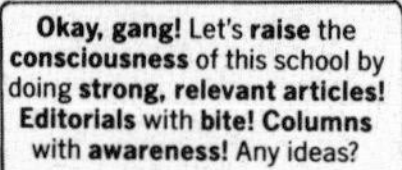

SEASONS

MISHAPS

SHOPPING

TRAVEL

SOCIAL ACTIVITY

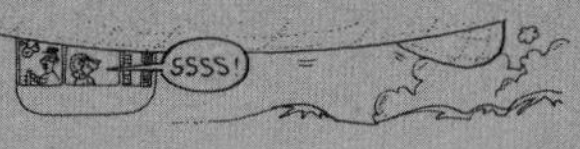

PERSUASION

SLEEP

CHOICES

B-S.A.T. DEPT.

Thinking about what career to get into? Wondering whether or not you'll fit in? Well, here's the fourth in a series of tests designed to help you choose your future line of work. Mainly, discover your true abilities by taking...

MAD'S APTITUDE TEST NUMBER FOUR

WILL YOU MAKE A GOOD POLITICIAN?

1. Complete this sentence. Once elected, a politician pushes to create new jobs for his ______________ .
   - A. Family
   - B. Cronies
   - C. Campaign contributors
   - D. All of the above.

2. When a candidate says he has an open mind about major issues, this usually means:
   - A. He can be bought by anyone.
   - B. Those reports that he's "wishy-washy" are true.
   - C. He's waiting to see the public opinion polls before he commits himself.
   - D. Any of the above.

3. As a politician, you attack your opponent with smears and innuendos. Is this a good practice?
   - A. Yes, if it's a close race and this is the only way you can get votes.
   - B. Yes, if you're trailing badly and want the perverse pleasure of destroying his character and reputation.
   - C. No, if you have an insurmountable lead and therefore can come off as a statesman.
   - D. Any of the above.

4. During a campaign, you hear your opponent advocate oil drilling on public land. How should you respond?
   - A. Call him an anti-environmentalist.
   - B. Say he's a tool of the big oil interests.
   - C. Label him a right-wing reactionary.
   - D. All of the above.

5. Your opponent changes his mind and now is *against* oil drilling on public land. How do you respond now?
   - A. Declare that he's keeping the U.S. dependent on foreign oil.
   - B. Say he's against creating thousands of new jobs.
   - C. Label him a bleeding-heart liberal.
   - D. All of the above.

6. When a Senator attacks "dishonesty in government," it's an indication that:
   - A. The other party is in and his is out.
   - B. His previous attack on "Creeping Socialism" didn't work.
   - C. It's a smoke screen to cover up what's being said about *him*.
   - D. Any of the above.

7. As a Congressman, you take a fearless, independent stand on a crucial bill. What does this mean?
   - A. You have a safe seat.
   - B. You're planning to retire, so what's the difference?
   - C. You meant to take the other side but, as usual, got confused.
   - D. Any of the above.

ARTIST: GEORGE WOODBRIDGE
WRITER: FRANK JACOBS

8. Like other politicians, this legislator prefers to speak on TV rather than make public appearances. Why?
   - A. The cue cards help him recall key facts, such as the name of his party.
   - B. The make-up prevents viewers from seeing he's over the hill.
   - C. He can edit in applause, cheers and appropriate fanfare.
   - D. All of the above.

9. As a politician, you support housing projects for the poor. What is your motive?
   - A. It packs them together in one place, preventing their spilling over into better neighborhoods—which goes over great with middle and high-income voters.
   - B. It shows you've got compassion, which goes over great with low-income voters.
   - C. It means big bucks to the building contractors who are contributing to your campaign.
   - D. All of the above.

10. Complete this sentence. When faced with a decision of conscience, a politician should do what's best for ______________ .
   - A. His re-election.
   - B. The most influential lobbyists.
   - C. His pocketbook.
   - D. All of the above.

SCORING

If you answered "D." to all the questions, you have the ability to make a great Politician.

ELECTION FRIGHT RETURNS DEPT.

It's been countless years of tortured, sleeples
nights since we last played our ghoulish gam
You might remember how it's played: we take

ARTIST: PAUL COKE

Digging Up A SCANDAL

Twisting A FACT

Ducking A QUESTION

Reviving An OLD ISSUE

Hanging On To A SLIM LEAD

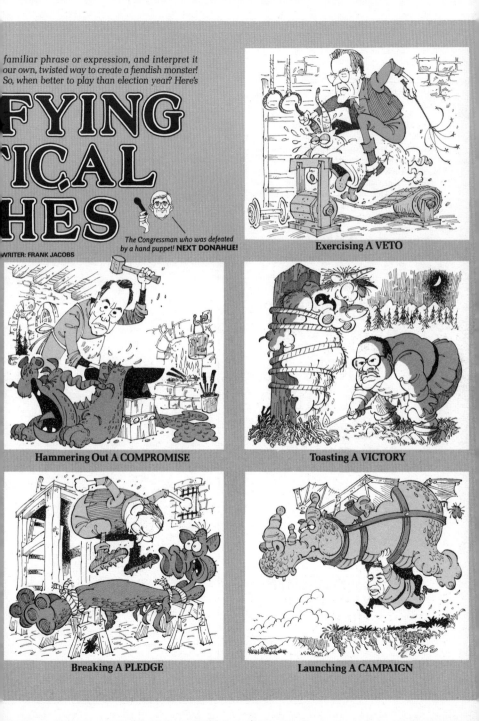

familiar phrase or expression, and interpret it our own, twisted way to create a fiendish monster! So, when better to play than election year? Here's

FYING 'ICAL HES

The Congressman who was defeated by a hand puppet! **NEXT DONAHUE!**

WRITER: FRANK JACOBS

Exercising A VETO

Hammering Out A COMPROMISE

Toasting A VICTORY

Breaking A PLEDGE

Launching A CAMPAIGN

SICK TRANSIT GLORIOUSLY DEPT.

Nowadays, Travel Agencies are packaging all kinds of tours for all kinds of people with all kinds of special interests, all designed to help them relax, leave their tensions behind and have a good time. But that doesn't make any sense. People work hard their whole lives developing their tensions, mainly in the form of their neuroses! Why should they want to give them up? The truth is...most people prefer to carry their neuroses with them! So why not design tours specifically for them? We'll show you what we mean with

THE MAD TRAVEL AGENCY'S SPECIALIZED TOURS FOR YOU AND YOUR NEUROSIS

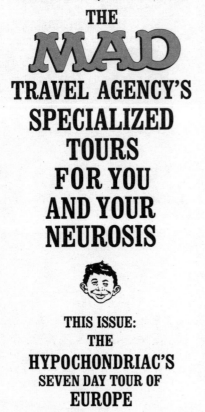

THIS ISSUE: THE HYPOCHONDRIAC'S SEVEN DAY TOUR OF EUROPE

ARTIST: HARRY NORTH, ESQ. WRITER: STAN HART

DAY 1

You leave Kennedy Airport, New York, at 8:00 P.M., just in time to be exposed to the unhealthy damp night air. You'll be seated next to two other tourists, and God only knows what germs they've been exposed to. While on board, you'll receive a head set for the movie, which might prevent you from hearing all the coughing and sneezing going on throughout the plane—but you'll know it's there. You'll be relieved to find that the utensils for your meals aloft are sealed in plastic bags, but the 6-hour flight will give you plenty of time to worry about whose filthy hands packed them inside the plastic bags.

DAY 2

You arrive in London and are whisked to your hotel overlooking the historic Thames River, the scene of the terrible London Plague of 1348. You'll spend the rest of the day at leisure, wondering if it was a "628-year-Plague," and it's time for it to return. You'll notice that the drinking glasses in your bathroom are wrapped in cellophane and marked "Sanitized For Your Protection." A little bit of British drollery there, since you know the maid only wipes the glasses with a dirty rag and shoves them into the cellophane. You'll also notice that the paper band over the toilet seat assures you that it, too, is "Sanitized For Your Protection"—probably with the same dirty rag used to wipe the glasses.

DAY 3 & 4

After a hearty breakfast of English sausage (which will give you gas and make you think you're having a heart attack), you'll be escorted to all the points of interest in London. You'll tour Buckingham Palace (but not get to see the Queen, since she's probably ill and they want to keep it a secret for political reasons). At the Tower of London and Westminster Abbey, you'll see where all the famous Englishmen are buried (which will be a wonderful reminder of how fleeting life really is, and that death is always lurking, even for the great). The changes in temperature going in and out of these wonderful landmarks will probably give you a chill, so you can spend the next day in bed, nursing a cold.

DAY 5

You fly to Paris. The flight takes less than an hour, but it's a great opportunity to take your temperature and compare symptoms with fellow passengers. In Paris, you'll be escorted to the famous Eiffel Tower, where someone already at the top will probably spit, and the germ-laden spittle will undoubtedly land on your head. You will then visit Notre Dame Cathedral where you can pray you'll get out of this infested country alive. At night, you'll be taken to Pigalle, where you'll surely contract a venereal disease from sitting on a toilet seat in the Crazy Horse Saloon.

DAY 6

You leave Paris (and not a moment too soon!) and arrive in Rome. First, you will visit the Colosseum, where the Christians were fed to the lions, and where you can sit and reflect upon how lucky they were to have died quickly instead of lingering on, like you're doing. Next, you'll visit St. Peter's and The Vatican, where you can arrange for a private audience with the Pope so you can pray together for God to restore your health. (Only the Pope doesn't look too well himself, so what's he going to do for a nobody like you? Besides, imagine what you're liable to get by kissing His Holiness's ring! Who knows who kissed it before you!) At night, you'll dine at the famous Alfredo's, where the highly-seasoned food will give you diarrhea, or constipation, or both.

DAY 7

You are transported by bus to the fabulous French Riviera. The bus is especially designed so the windows don't close completely, exposing you to the dangerous 75 degree temperature and probably giving you pleurisy. In your hotel, instead of the usual Gideon Bible at your bedside, you'll find a volume of "Symptoms Of Incurable Diseases Of Europe" for introspective reading. You can visit one of the many lavish gambling casinos, where you can play roulette and wonder what kind of people handled the chips before you. From Nice, you'll fly home with enough time aloft (8 hours) to worry if the U.S. Health Service will allow you to re-enter the country with all the diseases you picked up on your fabulously exciting trip to Europe.

NEXT ISSUE: THE PARANOI AC'S 7-DAY TOUR OF JAPAN

DON MARTIN DEPT.

ONE NIGHT IN A LIVING ROOM

CRASHING SYMBOLS DEPT.

Not too long ago, we confirmed the deaths of Mr. Clean, Charlie the Starkist Tuna and several other merchandising characters. It seems, however, that our list wasn't complete, and for MAD this won't do at all! Here, therefore, are *more*

OBITUARIES FOR MERCHANDISING CHARACTERS

ARTIST: BOB CLARKE WRITER: FRANK JACOBS

Noid Dies After Plot Fails to Pan Out

The Noid, longtime Domino's nemesis, died today after a failed attempt to sabotage the company's pizzas with tainted anchovies.

"It was clearly an act of revenge by a desperate creature," said a Domino's executive. "After we dropped him from our advertising campaigns, he vowed to get even. I guess he still wanted a slice of the pie."

It is believed that the Noid infiltrated an unheated oven, then was baked to death after it was turned on. He tried to escape, but was held fast by the melting cheese.

Funeral arrangements are being handled by Domino's, who promise to deliver him to his grave in less than 30 minutes.

NBC Peacock Dies

The NBC Peacock, 47, died today of poor exposure after failing to fight off an epidemic of cable-TV programs and video-cassette releases.

He will be replaced by a turkey.

Famed Party Animal Spuds MacKenzie Dies

Spuds MacKenzie, who electrified the nation with his beer drinking, carousing and gorgeous women, died today after being run over by a truck he was chasing. The Budweiser party animal had just turned six.

"He spotted a Miller Lite truck and went crazy," explained a Budweiser spokesman. "He was growling and snapping, determined to chase off the competition, but he got too close to the wheels. It's a great loss and we're as crushed as he is."

MacKenzie was hired by Budweiser as spokespooch in 1988, but not after some controversy. Several company executives feared he was giving the firm a black eye, and rumors persisted that he refused to be housebroken.

"Let's be fair to Spuds," the spokesman said. "Sure, he occasionally couldn't control himself at parties, but it's not easy holding all that beer."

MacKenzie will be buried on the company grounds, along with his leash, muzzle and diamond-studded collar. Pallbearers include Mighty Dog, Pluto, Snoopy, Marmaduke and McGruff, the Crime Dog.

Suicide Claims Life Of Exxon Tiger, 27

Suicide has claimed the life of the Exxon Tiger. He was 27.

The great cat, who inspired the slogan, "Put a tiger in your tank," was found in his locked garage with his motor running, a victim of carbon monoxide poisoning.

"I guess you could say it was a case of putting the tank in the tiger," joked an Exxon official.

According to friends, the Tiger had been extremely depressed ever since the Exxon oil spill in Alaska. As an endangered species, he was saddened by the loss of wildlife and felt ashamed of being the Exxon symbol.

"We'll probably stuff him and keep him as a trophy," said the Exxon executive, "or maybe use his hide as a slipcover."

The company has no plans to acquire another tiger. "Most likely, we'll come up with another animal as a symbol—like a snake or a vulture," the executive said. He is survived by a brother, Tony the Tiger.

Mr. Zip Dies at 36

According to a press release postmarked March 25, 1987, but received only today, Mr. Zip is dead after collapsing beneath several tons of junk mail. He was 36.

Energizer Rabbit Dies Of Digestive Disorder

The Energizer Rabbit died today of a digestive ailment, brought on by eating the burritos while interrupting a Taco Bell commercial.

"He couldn't resist the Mexican food," an Energizer spokesman said. "Within hours he was going and going and going. It wasn't a pretty sight! We tried to rush him into a Kaopectate commercial, but by then it was too late. He was going, going, gone!"

Mr. Peanut, 72, Dies In Mental Hospital

Mr. Peanut, longtime Planters employee, died yesterday at 72. He had been confined to a mental hospital, suffering from a severe identity crisis.

"He tried to put on rich, fancy airs with his top hat and monocle," said a company psychiatrist, "but deep down he knew he was only working for peanuts. He became terribly depressed, and despite years of therapy, we couldn't get him out of his shell. In the end, he was a certifiable nut case."

As of today, company officials had not decided whether to give him a funeral or a posthumous roast.

Smooth Character Dies After Missile Attack

Smooth Character, the humped symbol of Camel Cigarettes, has died of injuries suffered during a missile attack. He was 11.

According to a close friend, the Marlboro Man, the Smooth Character had been visiting relatives in Kuwait during Operation Desert Storm. He was struck by fragments of a Patriot Missile that had intercepted an incoming Scud.

"Actually his death is good for us," a Camel spokesman said today. "It proves beyond all doubt that smoking doesn't kill you, but missiles do."

Bluebonnet Girl, 41, Dies

The Bluebonnet Girl, 41, died today of exhaustion. Company officials blamed her death on an ever-increasing workload.

"It was clear she was spreading herself too thin," said a spokesman.

In accordance with her will, she will be cremated with her ashes scattered over all 50 states. "After all," she said recently, "everything's better with Bluebonnet on it."

Uncle Ben, 84, Dies In Racial Incident

Uncle Ben, 84, died today from injuries suffered in a racially motivated incident.

According to witnesses, he was stopped by Los Angeles police officers for no apparent reason. Though normally mild-mannered, Uncle Ben became stirred up and boiled over at the unlawful detainment, and a pressure-cooker situation quickly developed.

"We told him to put a lid on it," said one of the officers, "but he was in hot water from the start."

"No way," said Aunt Jemima, a neighbor. "Sure, he got steamed, but what they did to him goes against the grain."

Funeral arrangements are not complete, due to no one knowing Uncle Ben's religious preference. It is believed he was recently converted.

California Raisins Die of Old Age

The California Raisins, who sang and danced their way to national acclaim, have died of old age, according to news heard through the grapevine.

"It's not all that surprising," said Sun Maid, a close friend. "They were all dried up and wrinkled and feeling boxed in with age."

The group made their show-business debut as youngsters, calling themselves The Grapettes. Though green newcomers, they soon displayed the seeds of greatness. "A most pleasing bunch," said a local critic, who lauded them for their good taste.

As the years passed, however, the group appeared to run out of juice, forcing a major career change. "When they hung us out to dry, we gave our routine a new wrinkle," said one of the raisins last year, "and the fruit of our efforts paid off."

IT'S TRAINING CATS AND DOGS DEPT.

Hey, Letterman, you're missing a bet by showing only one si

Stupid Pet (

your pet trick schtick! We suggest you try MAD's...

wner Tricks

ATTA GIRL! CATCH THE CRUMBS!

NOW, THIS TIME LET'S TRY A HALF-GAINER WITH A TWIST!

ARTIST AND WRITER: PAUL PETER PORGES

GET READY, SWEETIE! SHRIEK, THEN JUMP ON THE CHAIR!

ROLL OVER, BIG FELLA!
PORGES

AN EMBARRASSMENT OF RICHARD'S DEPT.
A MAD PEEK BEHIND THE SCENES
ON THE SET OF A
SLASHER MOVIE
ARTIST: GREG THEAKSTON
WRITER: DICK DEBARTOLO
I still say we're going to get sued for this! It's too close to the classic Frankenstein story!
It's okay! I've given a whole new slant to the story. All this equipment is SOLAR powered! In this version, Frankenstein isn't waiting for a bolt of lightning, he's waiting for a really strong sunrise!
Besides, we've got it covered in the ads. We say our movie is "in the tradition of Frankenstein"! That's a nice way of saying we ripped off someone else's work!
I just met this girl for the first time in history class! What's my motivation for killing her an hour later?
40 million admission tickets at 6 bucks a head!
Sixteen different endings and I hate them all! Now what do we do?
Have a "write the ending" contest in Fangoria Magazine. Those fans will send us thousands of ideas and we use the best one and offer a big deal prize of $100!
FANGORIA
PROPS

NOW FILMING
ALFRAID VS GOOD TASTE
IT'S ALIVE
Wow! That's going to be a **shocker** on the screen! What a **scary make-up job!**
I wanted something **fresh!** People are **sick** of a **guy** in a **hockey mask** terrorizing a **summer camp!** We need to think **new!** How about a **girl** in a **football helmet** terrorizing an **Army camp?**
Well, the **reviews are in!** Listen to this from the New York *Times:* "A **senseless movie** with more **unprovoked violence** than we've **ever seen before.**"
MAKE-UP DEPT.
Inspired, M.H., really **quite inspired!**
Jerk, that's **Harriet Hasbeen,** and she **hasn't** been to make-up yet! Putting **old stars** in **horror films** is a great way for producers to get some big names **without** paying the **big bucks!**
ARMY
GOOD LUCK
Let's go over your **lines** to make sure you have them **memorized!**
Thanks! Here I go... **Yagghh...yaghh...help...! yaggh...yaggh...help...! yaggh...yaggh...help...! please, help!**
That's **nothing!** Listen to what the Los Angeles *Dispatch* said: "It's **wall-to-wall blood** and **unrelenting killing scenes.** There's absolutely **no story line** to follow. It's just **one gory murder** after another, **without rhyme** or **reason!"**
I **don't see** that third set of **yaggh's** in the script!
PANAVISION
PROM QUEEN
I **ad-libbed it!** I want to give a performance that's **fresh** and **creative!**
SOUND DEPT.
What a **break!** It's going to be an even **bigger hit** than we **thought!**
PROM NIGHT
Props, I think we need just a **touch** more **blood!**
Are you **sure?**
This is the **worst** horror film I **ever saw!** It's going to **die** at the **box office!**
Yes! Don't forget, this is the **romantic wedding scene!!!**
Who cares? We only made the movie so we could **sell mugs, tee-shirts, make-up kits, buttons** and **sweatshirts "based on the movie"!**
ALFRAID MAKE-UP KIT
ALFRAID 'N' SLASH
CUT!

JOKE AND DAGGER DEPT.

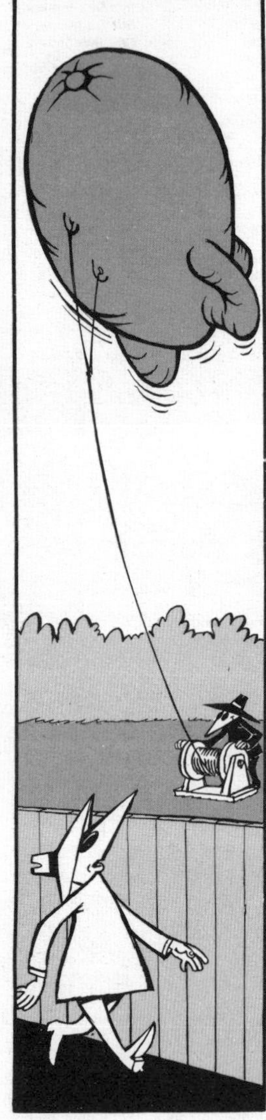

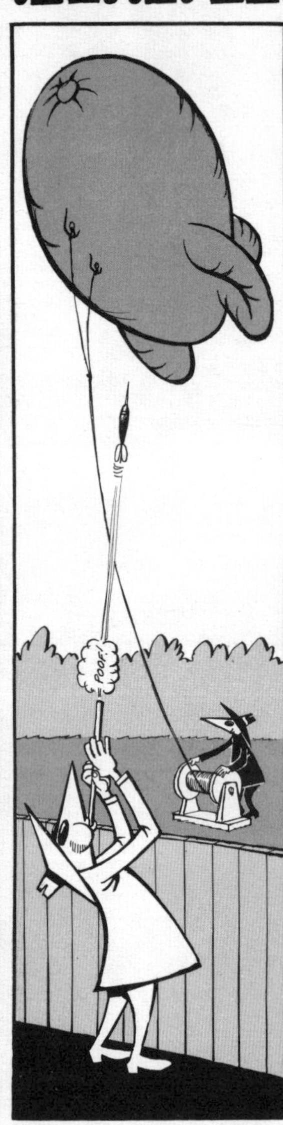

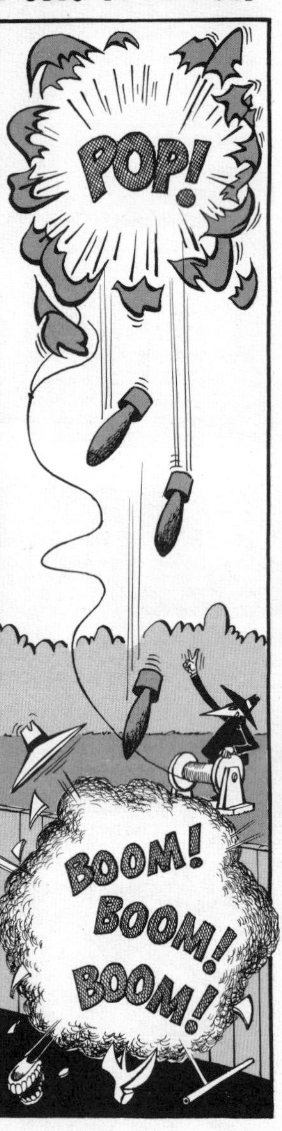

PROSE AND CONTEST DEPT.

MAD MAGAZINE READER'S COMPETITION

ENTRIES JUDGED BY: JOE RAIOLA AND CHARLIE KADAU

Results of Competition #1, *in which we asked you to create an appropriately titled outgoing phone message, one that people could leave on their answering machines to replace the dreadfully boring "I'm not in now, leave your name and number after the beep and I'll get back to you" style message.*

FIRST PRIZE OF A RARE COPY OF MAD #275 WITH THE MISSING CAPTION, REPORTED TO BE WORTH OVER $80,000 TO:

THE "JUST PLAIN SILLY" PHONE MESSAGE

"Hi, this is *(your name)*. At the moment I'm peach buffalo in squirming tub visiting hollow beverage. Trombone pleasantry? Noodle lengthening putty service of rewinding magnitude. Scrumptious tongue mystery hat. Tomahawk, tomahawk. Aluminum monkeys festering. You'll have 30 seconds to leave a message after the beep. Please speak clearly. (BEEEEEEP)

Submitted by: Doug Feeble, Gump, WI

SECOND PRIZE OF AN ALFRED E. NEUMAN TABLECLOTH KIT TO:

THE "HIGH TECH" PHONE MESSAGE

(To be spoken in a mechanical-sounding voice)

"Hello, you've reached *(your phone #)*. To leave a message for *(your name)*, press 1 now. If you wish to be called back, press 2 now. If your message will be one minute or longer, press 3 and 5 now. If your message will be under one minute, press 4, 7 and 8 now. If your message is extremely important and you can't wait any longer to leave it, press 6 nine times and 9 six times now. If you've been stupid enough to press any buttons during this totally useless recording, leave your message now!" (BEEEEEEP)

Submitted by: Louise Gummy, Pemberton Pines, VT

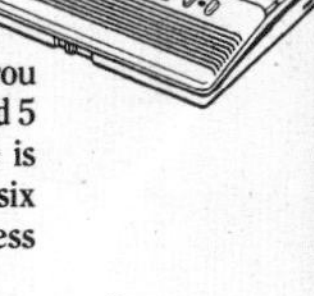

RUNNER-UP PRIZES OF A FIVE-MINUTE PHONE CALL FROM FRANK JACOBS TO:

THE "WHEN YOU DON'T WANT TO RETURN ANYONE'S CALL" PHONE MESSAGE

"Hi, this is *(your name)* and I'm not home now. After the beep, please leave your name, today's date, the time of your call, the phone number you can be reached at, the best times to call you, the temperature at the time of your call, your Social Security number, your feelings on the current trade deficit, your inseam measurement, your favorite film directed by Alan Parker, and your message. People failing to leave all of this information will not have their calls returned. You have 30 seconds." (BEEEEEEP)

Submitted by: Frederick Battering Ram-Simpson, Provo, UT

THE "EVERYBODY WANTS TO BE A MOVIE STAR" PHONE MESSAGE

"Hello, you've reached the *(your name)* Multiplex Theatre. Now showing in cinema one, "The Phone Message," an offbeat and disturbing adventure starring *(your name again)* as The Person Who's Never Home, with Sally Struthers as The Answering Machine, Joe Piscopo as The Dial Tone and introducing YOU as The Irate Phone Caller!" (BEEEEEEP)

Submitted by: Lee Cheechee Lee, Jr., Skankville, NY

And as in all our competitions, everyone who entered before the Nov. 15th, 1990 deadline receives a free one-year subscription to MAD. **Be sure to enter next time!**

BLIGHT UNSEEN DEPT.

At one time or another, you've probably seen a horse wearing blinders. Blinders are a good thing, because they keep the horse in a straight line and out of trouble, since it's unaware of what's going on around it. Sometimes, people are so unaware of what's going on around them, it seems like they're wearing blinders, too! It boggles the mind to consider how many lives could be changed for the better if someone would pull the blinders off these misguided souls and shout in their face...

"HEY-LO BE

ARTIST: AL JAFFEE

OOK HIND YOU!"

WRITER: MARK D'AMICO

THE WED MENACE DEPT.

A MAD LOOK AT

EDDINGS

ARTIST & WRITER: SERGIO ARAGONES

1
2
3
1
JUSTICE OF THE PEACE
2
3
JUSTICE OF THE PEACE
1
WITH LOVE AUNT AGATHA
2
?
1
2
3
CATERING SERVICES

5
JUST
MARRIED
4
ARAGONES

A MASSIVE CHART ATTACK DEPT.

Ever wonder about the correlation between seemingly unrelated events—between say, the number of crimes per 1000 households and the number of

CAUSE OR CO

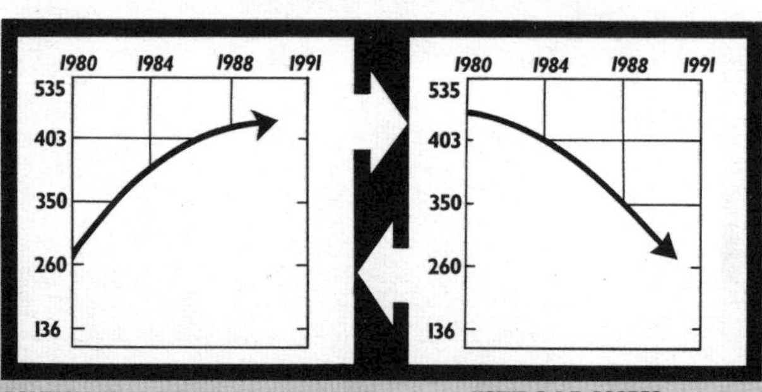

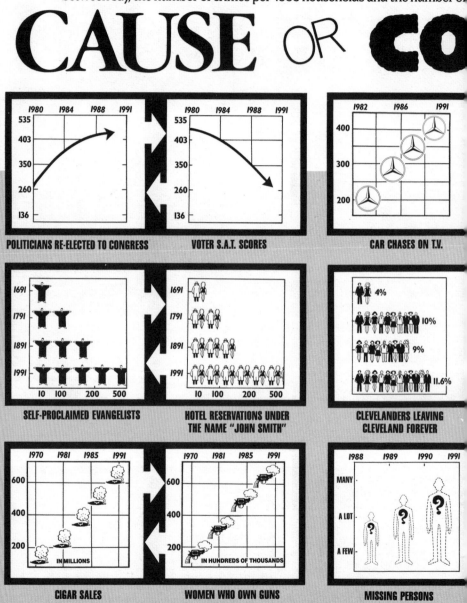

POLITICIANS RE-ELECTED TO CONGRESS

VOTER S.A.T. SCORES

1982 1986 1991
400
300
200

CAR CHASES ON T.V.

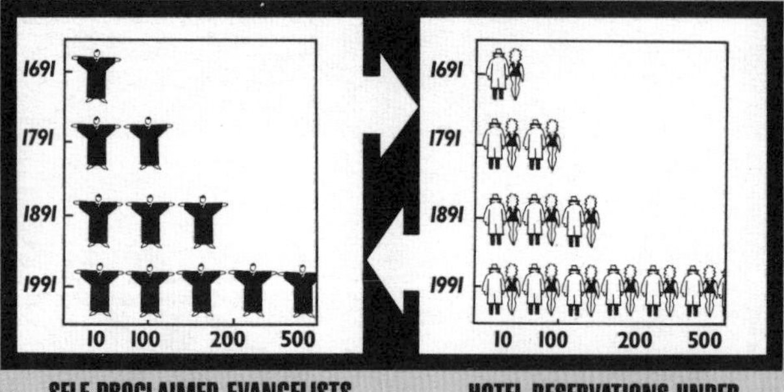

SELF-PROCLAIMED EVANGELISTS

HOTEL RESERVATIONS UNDER THE NAME "JOHN SMITH"

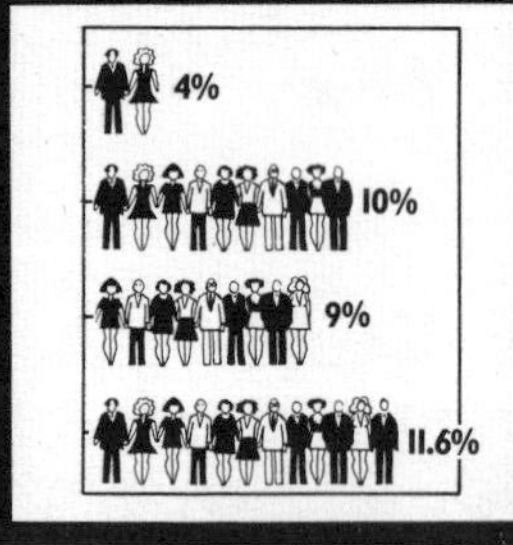

CLEVELANDERS LEAVING CLEVELAND FOREVER

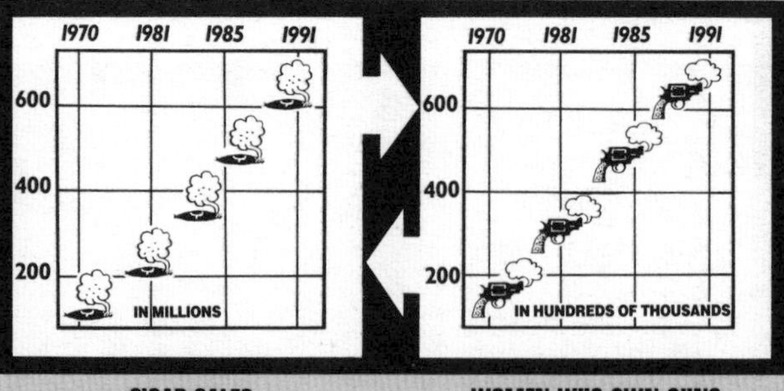

CIGAR SALES

WOMEN WHO OWN GUNS

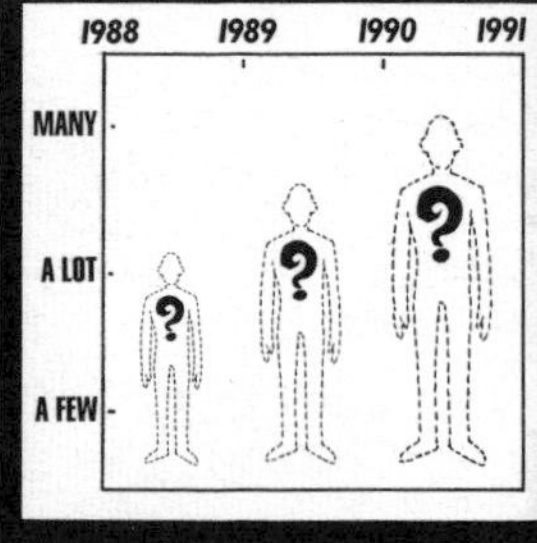

MISSING PERSONS

homes that display plastic snowmen? Is there a connection?? *Ummm*...no. But other statistical pairs *do* suggest definite links. You decide! Are they...

NCIDENCE??

ARTIST: GEORGE WOODBRIDGE WRITER: DAN BIRTCHER

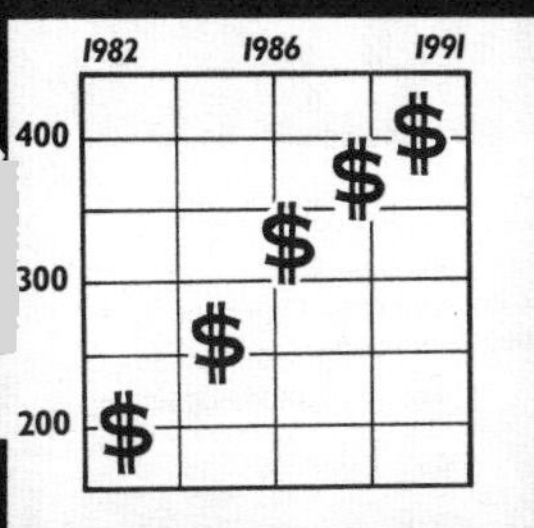

CAR INSURANCE PREMIUMS

GLOBAL WARMING

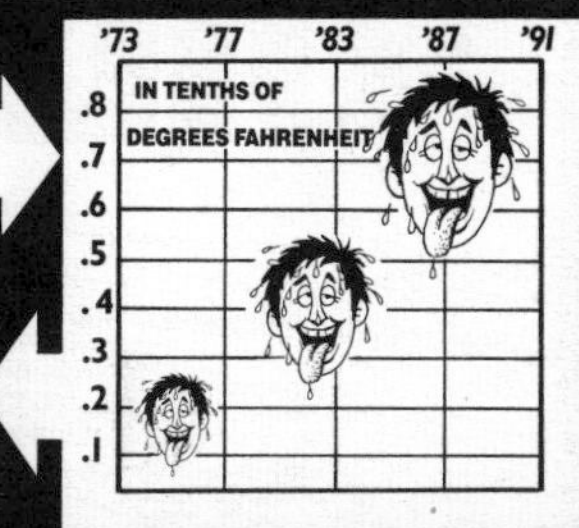

SALES OF X-RATED VIDEOCASSETTES

CLEVELANDERS WHO REALIZE THEY'RE IN CLEVELAND

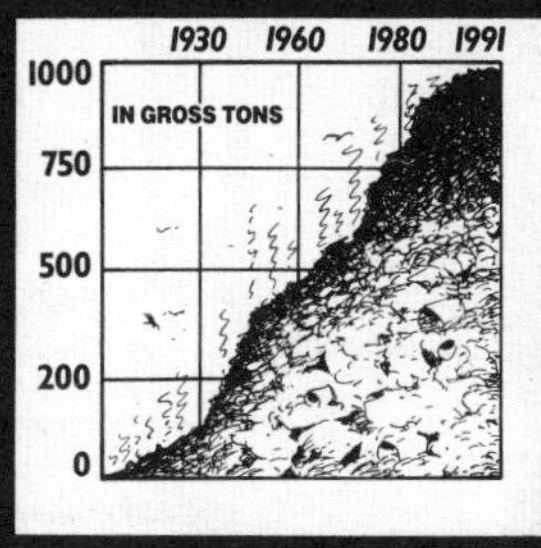

LANDFILL INCREASE

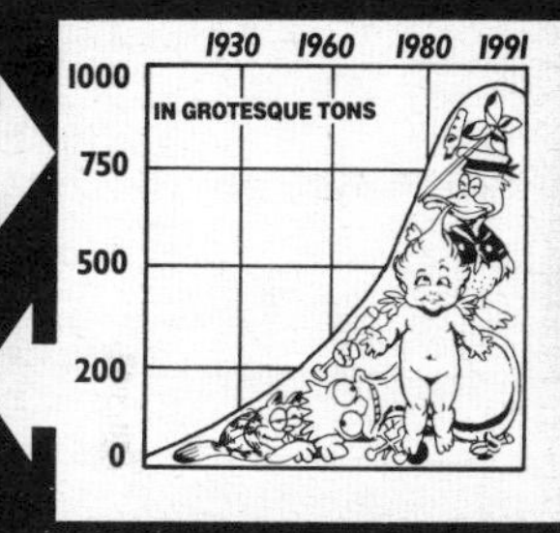

IMPORTS OF CRAPPY LITTLE CARNIVAL PRIZES

DAVID COPPERFIELD PERFORMANCES

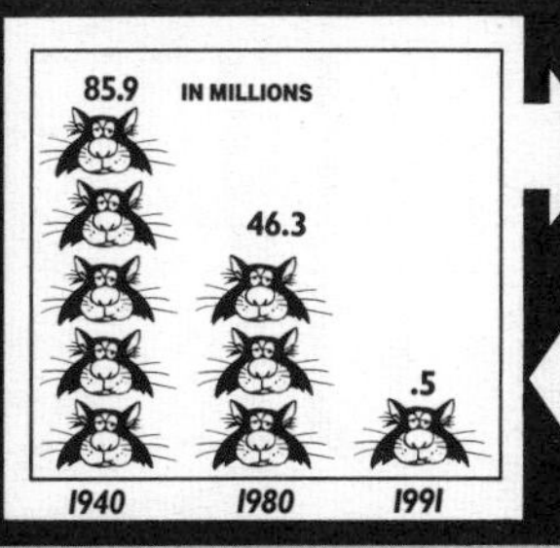

CAT POPULATION

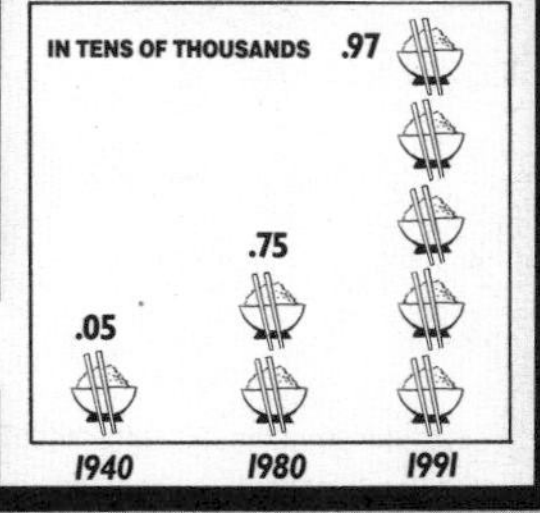

NUMBER OF CHINESE RESTAURANTS

FUNERAL DIRECTOR'S CUT DEPT.

These days, lots of people on the verge of taking the long dirt nap are opting for video wills. Why? We have no idea. Some say it's a more personal and touching way to bid farewell to their loved ones. But it's also dreadfully BORING watching the soon-to-be-very-dead person droning on about who gets their Kmart wristwatch and who gets their World's Fair coffee mug. They forget that video wills are *TV shows*! They need production values! Gimmicks! Flash! It is with this in mind that we present...

HOW TO SPICE UP YOUR VIDEO WILL

ARTIST: TOM BUNK WRITER: JEFF KRUSE

Provide a fun theme for your loved ones to enjoy.

Hire a young, sexy stand-in.

Do the whole thing in gangsta rap.

Speak in your own made-up language (except for a few names of family and friends) to keep them guessing as to who was left what.

Feature celebrity cameos.

Sprinkle in some product placement (which can also increase the amount of your heirs' inheritance).

Be sure to include bloopers and outtakes.

Include "pop-up" factoids, like on VH1.

Make it like a game show.

At the end, save a few minutes for Andy Rooney.

DON MARTIN DEPT.

ONE DAY WITH A WISHBONE